HOOSIER HYSTERICAL

HOW THE WEST BECAME THE *MID*WEST, WITHOUT MOVING AT ALL

By

Mark R. Hunter
with Emily Hunter

Other titles by Mark R. Hunter

Non-fiction:
Images of America: Albion and Noble County
Smoky Days and Sleepless Nights: A Century or So With the Albion Fire Department
Slightly Off the Mark: The Unpublished Columns

Fiction:
Storm Chaser
Storm Chaser Shorts
The Notorious Ian Grant
The No-Campfire Girls

Photos by Mark R. Hunter & Emily Hunter except where noted

Edited by Emily Hunter

Cover by Emily Hunter

This book is a work of nonfiction. While every effort was made to keep the facts as straight as possible, this is a humor book, and isn't meant to be taken as a scholarly work ... unless some school is foolish enough to want five hundred copies, in which case we'll arrange a different disclaimer for their edition. This is meant to be a work of satire and humor, and maybe even is. Leaving your sense of humor at home before reading it is just as dangerous as making an hour and three quarter speech on a cold March day without a coat or hat, and just look how that worked out for William Henry Harrison.

For book extras and additional books by the author, please visit:
www.MarkRHunter.com

HOOSIER HYSTERICAL

HOW THE WEST BECAME THE *MID*WEST, WITHOUT MOVING AT ALL

By

Mark R. Hunter
Emily Hunter

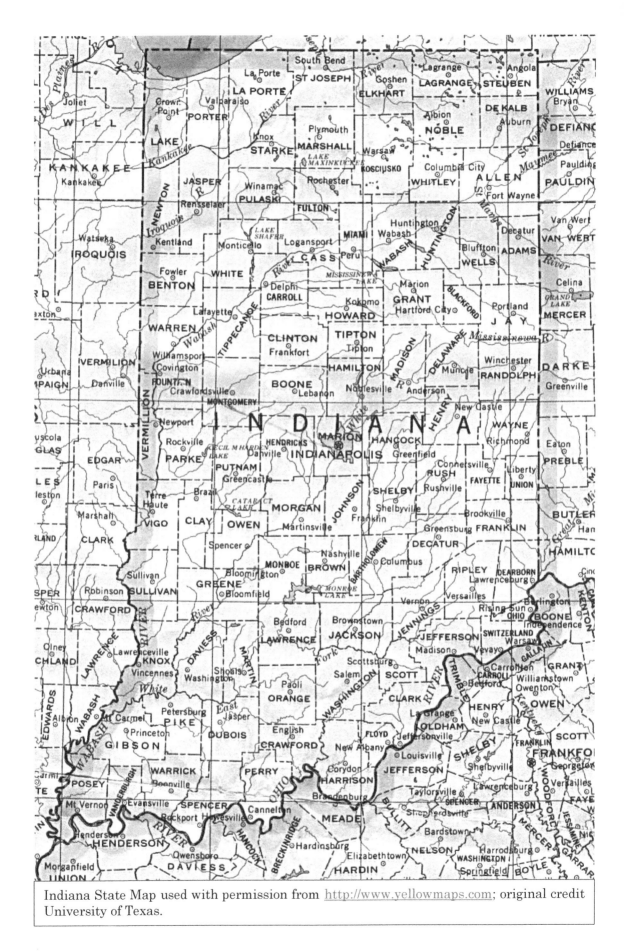

Indiana State Map used with permission from http://www.yellowmaps.com; original credit University of Texas.

Forward

THE PART WHERE I EXPLAIN MYSELF

No book about anything, including the boring ones and the really badly written ones, would be possible without the contribution of people other than the writers. Writers sometimes acknowledge this, in sections we like to call "acknowledgements".

I'd like to thank Steve Jobs, who created a kick-ass computer system I can't afford, and Bill Gates, who sells a not-too-bad word processing program to use on the computer system I *can* afford. Without people like them, I'd still whack away at a manual typewriter while trying to remember typesetter correction symbols.

More than that I'd like to thank my wife, who did not roll her eyes when I suggested doing a humorous history of Indiana. Well, not when I could see her. If this works out, I'll do a similar book about every state with a Native American connection to its name: Delaware, Mississippi, Michigan ... um, Massachusetts ...? Who thought naming a state Massachusetts was a good idea? Elementary school kids there must spend all of second grade learning to spell one word. They should have named it New Pilgrim.

Most of all I'd like to thank, naturally, American Indians, who loaned their name to our fair state that could otherwise have been Hoosieria. Of course, it wasn't their idea ... and it wasn't their real name. But it was still nice of them.

The problem with history isn't that it's not interesting; it's that it's not *made* interesting. For instance, all too often history classes stress memorizing dates, although I must admit those are the only dates I got in high school. Many Americans take pride in their hatred of math, which I'm sure has nothing at all to do with our decline as a nation. Dates are numbers, and dates are only important when compared to other dates, and voila: math.

Similarly, old dusty statues are of interest only to birds, and certain types of birds, at that. (I have a Hoosier friend named Neil Case who's an expert birder—which is a real word. Maybe I'll ask him which birds prefer marble bathrooms.)

Years ago, under Mayor Bloomberg, New York City embarked on an extensive plan to potty train birds. They were going specifically for pigeons, but it turns out there are 476 species of wild birds documented in New York, and each has different bathroom habits. Some liked the lid up, some down, some preferred the toilet paper roll under, some over ... the effort failed completely. Bloomberg moved on to a program of feeding birds more nutritious food. This had no effect on how much poop ended up on statues.

Let's face it: Nobody wants to look at a poopy statue.

No, the way to interest people in history is to show how history was made by real people, who faced real problems, just like people who make history today. Did you know second President John Adams suffered irritable bowel syndrome? It's why his cabinet meetings broke up so quickly. That also explains why he's regarded as the grouchiest of the Founding Fathers.

Here's another fun fact you've probably already heard: Adams died on the 50th anniversary of our nation's founding. His last words? "Thomas Jefferson survives."

Unfortunately, Jefferson died five hours earlier. To this day Adams' ghost haunts Boston, asking for a last-words do-over, and complaining about how long it takes for kids to learn how to spell Massachusetts.

Interestingly, John's cousin, Sam Adams, was the first person to say "You can have my gun when you take it out of my cold hands!" That's the original quote, by the way, without the word "dead"; it was winter. Later Sam Adams invented beer, and never again complained of cold hands.

That's interesting stuff.

Indiana's motto is "The Crossroads of America", largely because it has a lot of roads, which tend to cross each other. (More interstate per square mile than any other state. Is that something to brag about?) This is despite the fact that, with the exception of Hawaii, Indiana is the smallest state west of the Appalachian Mountains. Perhaps it's compensating for something.

As hinted at earlier, the name Indiana is thought to mean "Land of Indians", for reasons that are probably obvious. Presently the capital of the state is the imaginatively named Indianapolis. "Polis" is a Greek word for city, or city-state. Thus, Indianapolis is the city of Indiana. We're a plainspoken people.

On an unrelated note, "Acropolis" means high city. So does "Denver".

So sit back and learn something fun about history. When you're done, read this book.

The actual, honest-to-goodness crossroads of America
Max Ehrmann is best known for his famous poem, "Desiderata".
Um … no, I haven't read it. Still, he was famous enough that a life sized statue of Ehrmann sits on a bench at the junction of 7th and Wabash streets in Terra Haute, where he often sat to write. It was a busy place, also known as the intersections of US 40, the National Highway, and US 41, one of the first major north-south routes in America. It was, quite literally, one of the first crossroads of America. In fact, that's the site's nickname.
That doesn't seem like a quiet place for poetry writing, but still.

Chapter One:
THE PART THAT COMES FIRST

You Don't Have To Go To Indiana to Find Indians

Shelter is one of the top priorities for a new settler. However, contrary to popular belief, the first humans to enter Indiana did not build a Motel 6. They built a Motel 1. After all, they had to start somewhere. It happened as early as 8000 BC, with the twelfth tribe out of Alaska, or possibly the thirteenth tribe out of Israel.

Modern scientists call these first settlers Paleo-Indians, and they're the only ones who can honestly say they didn't steal the place from someone else ... except possibly Paleo-armadillos. (Look it up—they were huge.) It's possible they even came from India, or at least came through India at some point. Just the same, you'd think a more accurate name would be Paleo-Siberians.

Some say the Paleo-Indians arrived as much as 10-12 thousand years ago, right after they settled on the term Paleo-Indians. The time for arrival in the Americas is always being pushed back. Some say Columbus actually got here hundreds of years before 1492, on a Viking River Cruise.

So the Native Americans were not native. This irony doesn't matter in the scheme of things, since they found no one there to kick out (depending on which ancient mysteries conspiracy theory you subscribe to). They lived in North America for thousands of years, before ultimately being overwhelmed by illegal immigrants (or, as we like to call it, being supplanted by civilization).

The newcomers arrived by way of a land bridge that connected Siberia with Alaska, although of course they weren't called Siberia and Alaska at the time. For the settlers to willingly brave the cold and the polar bears, things in Asia must have been pretty darned lousy. But eventually some of them made their way to Central America, discovered chocolate, and lived in paradise until the arrival of the aforementioned civilization.

Others took a wrong turn while circling Indianapolis, and boy, is *that* easy to do. They settled in the Midwest, imported corn from the much happier natives of Central America, and the rest is history. The latter natives actually called the crop maize, and this is how modern misspelled corn mazes became so popular.

Some of the newcomers were a little ... unusual. Ancient graves have been discovered of abnormally tall people, so much so they're often called giants. This led, of course, to the phrase "corn fed" to describe tall people. Researchers later determined corn alone won't account for unusual growth, which lead to the theory that mastodons were tasty. Oh, and before you get any ideas, mastodon hunting has been banned on the grounds of Indiana University-Purdue University Fort Wayne. (Obscure college joke, there—the IPFW mascot is the Mastodon.)

Early natives left great mounds all around Indiana and neighboring states. The purpose of those mounds remained a puzzle, until a twelve year old boy from Clarksville pointed out the natives seemed to have no outhouses. This came as a tremendous shock to archeologists of the time, who were known to be very hands-on.

(You've heard of Clarksville, Indiana; it's where the last train went to.)

Mastodon ... Science!

A mastodon stands guard over Science Central, a kid-centric world of wonder in the 1929 Fort Wayne City Light and Power Plant ... which, just to be clear, is no longer a power plant. How do I know it's a mastodon and not a mammoth? Easy: Indiana University-Purdue University Fort Wayne placed dozens of these variously decorated statues around the city, and the IPFW mascot happens to be the Mastodon.

The original natives became, of course, hunters. They had to be: There was no Steak n' Shake, no Essenhaus, no Original Pancake House, no pancakes at all. It was truly the dark culinary ages. Don't even get me started on Dog n' Suds.

Later they would turn to gathering, in addition to hunting, but in the early years the concept of storage units had not yet caught on. Still, they had animals for food; that also gave them clothing, on the assumption that once dead, the animals wouldn't need their skins anymore. Attempts to use animal bones to build homes didn't work too well, but a few tall sticks and some skins gives you a tent.

Later they hunted smaller animals, which led to smaller skins, which led to both sewing and the invention of the bikini.

Then the first Pottery Barn arrived, and with pottery Native Hoosier life changed forever.

Good Eats: A Maize in a Basket Case

The good news is, the first settlers in Indiana found all sorts of tasty meals: wolves, bears, saber-toothed tigers, mammoths, and beaver with nasty attitudes and giant overbites.

(Or maybe the mammoths were actually mastodons. No one ever got brave enough to ask.)

The bad news is, all of those meals started out alive. They didn't want to die. In fact, they were insulted by the idea of providing these newcomers with food and clothing. "What, we get here first, and then you want to poke us with sticks?" They didn't literally say that because—animals. Maybe if they had, it would have scared off the non-native natives.

Humans arrived with spears and motivation, the motivation coming from the fact that the means to carry supplies with them had not yet been invented. Have you ever tried to go on an extended vacation using nothing but old Wal-Mart bags? They didn't even have the bags. So they hunted big game, cooked them over open fires, and after that first winter saved every bit of animal fur for clothing and shelter. Their idea of central heating was to gather around the fire, exchanging stories about who got the biggest mastodon that day.

Soon they started to hunt smaller animals. This idea began in 1400 B.C. with Sig "One-Arm" Ugg and his partner, Yok "Scar Face" Sorgenson.

They decided after a particularly exciting bear hunt that maybe they didn't want to hunt bear anymore, and led the switch to small game. Ironically, Sig expired the next spring after encountering a particularly grouchy groundhog, which had just discovered they were scheduled to suffer six more weeks of winter.

Rabbits and deer became the new targets. The natives were particularly motivated to hunt deer, which they came to hate; the deer developed a nasty habit of jumping out in front of the hunters as they ran after bigger game, causing sometimes painful man-deer accidents.

Eventually, to put a little distance between them and tasty animals that all too often liked to taste back, humans invented the bow. At some point after that, having discovered throwing a bow wasn't very effective, they invented arrows.

The Indians—and I use that term to differentiate them from the next wave of immigrants—also caught fish from lakes, rivers, and streams, of which Indiana has lots. They ate shellfish and mussels in such large amounts that mounds of shells were sometimes found next to those other mounds, where an entirely different type of waste product accumulated. Whenever archeologists found twin mounds, they would flip a coin to decide who searched which mound first. Whoever came up with shells was the winner.

Oh, deer

You can't drive in Indiana without living in fear of encountering at least one deer, like this one hitchhiking near Angola. Modern residents will be shocked to learn Hoosier deer were hunted almost to extinction in the early 1900s. The animals were reintroduced to the state in the 1930s—only hunters can understand why—and modern hunting programs started up in the 50s.

Now it's believed the deer population is actually higher than before Europeans arrived, partially due to agriculture (yummy food) and the elimination of natural predators (fewer teeth).

They (the Indians, not the archeologists) later became gatherers, collecting fruits and nuts long before the white man gathered fruits and nuts into political assemblies.

Eventually the Indians figured out that certain seeds could be planted, and those seeds would grow into plants. If you harvested those plants, your kids would have something to complain about at dinner time. They engineered wild plants into crops like corn, pumpkins, beets, squash, and tomatoes. So we have them to thank for corn and tomatoes, and to blame for beets and squash.

When the crops came in, the Indians would store them in big piles on the ground. That's when the animals they hunted would sneak in and get their revenge. Then the insects would come in (insects didn't care about revenge, but they knew a good squash from a bad one).

It's not known who first came up with the idea to slap clay together into a bowl shape and then burn it until it got hard enough to hold food and drink. Throughout history there have been people who get pointed at a lot, until their crazy ideas work out. All we know is that at some point some Steve Jobs came up with the crazy idea, and later on some Bill Gates got even nuttier and did the same thing with copper. Thus was invented the first iBowl.

After that, American Indians began to live together in villages. Well, more permanent villages—the ones they had before were the ancient equivalent of RV parks.

Now they had a stable food supply, and no longer needed to forage and travel with the seasons. That left them time to organize into nations, form committees, pass parking regulations—and believe me, you've never seen an angry mammoth until you've seen one with a parking ticket slapped on its tusk. It was all downhill from there.

On the brighter side, the stability and time allowed trading to start between the villages. If one village didn't have enough corn, they'd get it from another village. If one village had too many beets, they were pretty much out of luck.

Soon two major Indian groups lived east of the Mississippi River: The Iroquois, who had enough beets, and the Algonquian, who had too many. The Algonquians eventually died out, as their children rebelled against their beet breakfasts and went to the other side.

As if that wasn't bad enough, some of the Iroquois discovered if they boiled maple sap long enough, it became maple syrup. They were overjoyed, until they realized they had no pancakes. The concept of syrup covered beets was not an idea whose time had come.

Eventually a new wave of people came through, and found Indiana to be a great place to grow crops—something they'd have known earlier if they just asked the American Indians. Indiana has become the third largest soybean producer and the fourth largest corn producer in the country, which is pretty impressive for the 38th largest state.

Indiana's also big into hogs, cattle, and chicken production. This, at times, doesn't give us the most attractive atmosphere, at least downwind. But it sure makes for some great breakfast meals, especially since we still also produce a lot of maple syrup. Thank goodness for pancakes.

And beets? No longer on the top 20 list.

(I know I'm being hard on beets. In fairness, let's remember beets saved many an American Indian from hunting, where they might gain the nickname "One Arm".

280-year-old newcomers

In 1734 Jesuit missionaries visited the village of Vincennes, and fourteen years later raised a small church. That led to this in 1826: the St. Francis Xavier Cathedral and Library, now known as The Old Cathedral. It's near the George Rogers Clark National Historical Park, along the unsurprisingly named Church Street.

So this building, declared a cathedral in 1834, serves the oldest Catholic parish in Indiana. I don't mean the individual members … well, I haven't done a survey. In 1970 Pope Paul VI elevated it from a Cathedral to a Basilica, and four Bishops are buried there. As if that wasn't enough, the library part, which began with the collection of Bishop Brute, was the first library established in Indiana.

Indiana Stats:

Facts is Facts

Well, you have to assume these facts are true, don't you? I mean, how do you really know? Are you going to drive around the state with a ruler and a calculator, and check them personally?

Just doing my part to promote modern paranoia.

Indiana became a state on December 11, 1816, after the inhabitants of the other eighteen states kicked out anyone who chewed tobacco, walked outside barefoot, or used the word "Hoosier". Eventually the first two habits worked their way back into the rest of the country, especially when Southern states were admitted. Well, how many Minnesotans walk around barefoot? (As for Hoosier, that word will get a whole chapter of its own. Jealous, Buckeyes? I haven't even given you a book.)

Why did we start in December? Well, there was nothing else to do. At that time people made their own presents, so the Christmas shopping season wasn't a factor.

As of the turn of the century (this one, not the last one), the population of Indiana was 6,114,745 ... 6 ... 7 ... oops, 4 ...

The highest point in Indiana is 1,257 feet above sea level, in Wayne County. This is a measure of distance. The ongoing rumor that the people in Wayne County choose to stay high because their neighbors are Ohio is a dastardly rumor, possibly started by pot smokers in Denver. Actually, the people of Colorado laugh at the thought of us being high, in every sense of the word.

I'm not sure if it's in the purview of this book to make fun of other states. This is mostly because I have no idea what purview means.

The lowest point in Indiana is in Posey County, which is way down in the southwest corner and thus, like the highest point, qualifies in more ways than one. It's at 320 feet, so we're still safe from rising sea levels. It is *not* safe from the Ohio River.

Perhaps ironically, the county seat of Posey County is Mount Vernon. The county was named after General Thomas Posey, who was Governor of the Indiana Territory and so got naming rights. He grew up next to George

Posey County Courthouse

All the way down in the very southwestern most corner of Indiana, hemmed in by the Ohio and Wabash Rivers, is the county named for Revolutionary War General and Indiana Territory Governor Thomas Posey. He's the one who renamed the Posey County Seat after Mount Vernon. The town's former name was McFaddin's Bluff, so perhaps Posey should be thanked.

The county courthouse was built in 1876, and designed by architect Levi S. Clarke—no relation to George Rogers Clark.

Washington's house at Mount Vernon, and rumor had it Posey was Washington's illegitimate son. It could be Posey was a poser.

Sorry, I hit a low spot and veered off on a tangent.

Indiana was once home to elk and bison, giant animals last seen in the state around 1830. No one who ever hit a deer in the Hoosier state— which includes almost everyone who ever drives here—is shedding any tears over the loss of any bigger animals.

Don't even start me on the woolly mammoth, which died out due to a warming climate when wool got too hot.

The largest limestone deposit in the world can be found in southern Indiana, which ships it all over for construction. In the mid-1800s the English Navy, mistakenly mixing up "limestone" with "lime", ordered a large shipment to help their sailors ward off scurvy. The order was canceled after the first three ships sank.

I mentioned earlier that Indiana is the smallest contiguous state west of the Appalachian Mountains, which themselves are the largest chain of mountains east of the Rockies. I don't know if that last is true, but it looks good on a map. Still, at 35,867 square miles, Indiana is the 38th largest state. This is because so many of the earlier, eastern states are so old they've shrunk. Clearly Rhode Island got washed on hot.

Another interesting fact is that the first professional baseball game was played in Fort Wayne, which is Indiana's second largest city, has three rivers, and has been owned by four different countries if you include the original tenants. This series of numbers is a statistical coincidence, but statistical coincidences can be fun.

Chapter Two:
EUROPEAN ARRIVALS, OR: HOW TO RUIN A GOOD THING

A lot of Indian tribes migrated through Indiana (ironically before it became Indiana). Sometimes they stayed; sometimes they went on to search for places with smaller mosquitoes. Experts say the original tribes include the Shawnee; the Illini, who later moved west and to this day sometimes vote in Chicago; and the Miami, who came north after a particularly bad hurricane season.

Some of the smaller or more temporary tribes have names that live on today. For instance, the Pokagon Band of the Potawatomi lends its name to a state park, while the Delaware had an Indiana county and a Delaware state named after them. Muncie is now a city in Indiana, and Kickapoo gets made fun of a lot. Remember, "Kickapoo" wasn't giggle-inducing in its original language. If you go through an Indiana map today, you'll find a large percentage of place names come from either the natives or the Revolutionary War.

But that would come later. The first Europeans came along in the early 1600s, and since the Revolution didn't break out for another 150 years or so, mapmakers held off.

Around 1614 a very polite man by the name of Samuel de Champlain showed up. He'd founded Quebec in what would become Canada, and was governor of New France in what would not become New France.

Champlain made the first accurate coastal map of Canada, and also had a drink named after him. Unfortunately, he finished several of those drinks before thinking to name them, and ended up misspelling his own name. As a result, he never got the credit he deserved for champagne. Upset by that, and also freezing, he headed south and became the first European to explore the Great Lakes area. So much for booze never being good for anything; thanks to Champlain Indiana became part of New France, with the promise that the French Empire in North America would go on for a long, long time.

And we all know how well that worked out.

However, the first white man to set foot in Indiana itself is believed to be Robert Cavalier Sieur de La Salle, whose name I'll shorten to La Salle for obvious reasons. He arrived in New France in the lucky year of 1666, with the intention of exploring lands no one had ever seen before. This came as quite a surprise to the people already there.

La Salle's group sailed across Lake Michigan, then reached the southern shore and the St. Joseph River, which I'm pretty sure had different names at the time. They ended up camped on the south bend of the St. Joseph, which became the imaginatively named city of South Bend.

Later he discovered the Mississippi River and claimed the whole area for France, naming it after King Louis. So Indiana was once part of Louisiana. Yet, do we get nice weather in winter? Do we get to celebrate Mardi Gras? Nah.

Vigo? It's not an Indian name

The Vigo County Courthouse is the spot where Joseph Smith held meetings to defend his fledgling religious movement, the Latter Day Saints. The county's namesake, Revolutionary War hero Francis Vigo, left money in his will for a courthouse bell, and in 1884 work started on the present structure—which looks pretty darned imposing, even surrounded by fast food joints.

The first fort built in the state, around 1715, was Fort Miami, continuing the southern connection. And yet no one ever goes there for spring break, possibly because of its intimidating modern name: Fort Wayne.

It was another fort, further south, that became the oldest settled town in Indiana. Again, this depends on the opinions of the Indians, who had lots of villages. None of them, old or new, boasted a single Starbucks, so the definition of civilized remains in the air.

At the time the French were into fur trading, which wasn't looked down upon nearly to the extent it is now. People froze to death a lot more often back then. So in 1732 they established a fur trading post, along with a fort built by a guy named Vincennes. My fingers are too tired to type the rest of his name. Oh, what the heck: It's Francois-Marie Billot, Sieur de Vincennes. Guess they had more time for signatures back then.

Eventually the Chickasaw Indians captured and burned de Vincennes,

Grist for the Mill

One early settler was Squire Boone, who around 1790 wandered Indiana with his little known brother, Daniel Boone. They spent some time hiding in a cave from the people who already lived there, then in 1808 Squire returned to buy the surrounding land and start a grist mill. The two are connected: a stream exits the nearby cavern and powers an 18 foot wheel, which turns thousand pound stones that grind corn into meal and grits. After being damaged by fire in the 1920s the mill was restored, and includes original foundation stones with carvings by Squire. It operates just the way it did when first built, which is more than I'll be able to say after two centuries. Yes, you can buy its products ... grits for breakfast?

down in Mississippi—what's this thing about connections with the south, anyway? The town and fort on the Wabash River were renamed Vincennes in his honor, but you've got to figure he'd have preferred to become immortal by not dying.

During the French and Indian War the British Empire—which didn't even get their name in the war's title—took over Vincennes and named the post Fort Sackville. Thankfully, the new name didn't stick.

Vincennes' story wasn't done, there: the village later became capital of the Indiana Territory. It lost out on being the first capital of the state due to its remote location, which makes you wonder why they bothered with it to begin with.

Indian Wars II: Attack of the Germs

It's a fantasy to think Native Americans were a simple, peaceful people before Europeans arrived. Believe me, they could pick a fight as well as anyone. (But why believe me?) Just the same, the French, British, Spaniards, and Luxembourgians brought more with them than just a few germs and viruses.

(Luxembourg explorers never got to the Midwest because, well ... they didn't own any boats. They did, however, once fight a war with Switzerland over a strayed flock of mountain goats.)

American Indians initially welcomed Europeans to the Midwest, because of vague promises involving Pop Tarts and flat screen TVs. When the newcomers showed up with blankets and colored glass beads, their hosts weren't too happy. Still, they also brought knives, guns, and iron pots. Have you ever tried to fry a rabbit on a wooden skillet? Or cook a nice beet soup with a woven grass pot? I didn't think so.

Here is a partial transcript from an early French trader meeting the natives, done by a Native stenographer:

"I'd like to present you *cough* with this flintlock musket and *hack* really cool glass beads that you can watch until you get cable *cough* *cough*."

"Dude, are you okay? Would you like some pine bark tea?"

"No, no ... *cough* ... just beet allergies ..."

While some have questioned whether that transcript is authentic, there can be no doubt American Indians had no natural immunity to things like smallpox, measles, and cooties. They died by the thousands, and the glass beads didn't do crap to help.

Meanwhile, English settlers began to make their way over the Appalachian Mountains. "Appalachian" is a Mohican term meaning "That'll keep them out for a while". It only delayed the English, who weren't all that interested in trading with the natives anyway. The French were more into travel by water, so between the Mississippi and Ohio Rivers and the Great Lakes, anyone with a canoe and a fur hat got in. Allons-y!

In the early 1700s the English started arriving, which prompted the French to send in soldiers. After all, the place was still called New France. The French warned the Indians that if they traded with the English, the French would attack them.

Meanwhile, the English warned the Indians that if they traded with the French, the English would attack them.

You could say the Indians got trapped between a rocky mountain chain and a wet place.

When the French and Indian War broke out in 1755 most of the Indians fought with the French, who had the advantage of having already been there for a while. They had the disadvantage of being the French, already honing their national talent for getting beaten.

Okay, in fairness the French were outnumbered and short on supplies. They signed a treaty, which turned over all the French lands east of the Mississippi, and Canada, to the English. The English now owned all the Midwest, which was then called the West.

The Native Americans, who you might remember lived there and had done so for hundreds of years, said: "Wait—what? Huh?"

But at least the King of England did one thing for them: He banned the English colonists on the East Coast, which was then called the East Coast, from settling west of the Appalachian Mountains. That made the Indians happy.

Obviously, their experience level with laws and treaties was still early in the learning curve.

Don't go up that creek, especially without a paddle

There's nothing so relaxing as a boat ride across a calm lake, assuming you don't get attacked by a giant turtle, or the British army—and that almost never happens these days. Here a family cruises on Worster Lake, at Potato Creek State Park.

Indiana Facts:
WEATHER OR NOT

Indiana cannot lay claim to the saying, "If you don't like the weather, wait five minutes". But we do anyway.

The problem with making fun of Indiana weather is that we're not the coldest, hottest, wettest, or driest state. You can't stop a blizzard at the Michigan state line—boy, I wish we could—and you can't make a tornado in Illinois turn away before it reaches Gary. No, Indiana's weather isn't more *anything* than the surrounding states.

But we say it is.

On the other hand, the weather isn't any *less* anything than the surrounding states. Okay, so we don't set cold weather records like Minnesota does ... is that a bad thing?

We do have "fun" with extremes. The average annual rainfall, so says the Indiana State Climate Office, is 40 inches. That's great, but sometimes we get it all in one day.

(Actually, in one day in 1905, 10.5 inches fell in Princeton. And to think, they never thought they'd use those swimming lessons.)

The average first freeze date is October 16, and the average first day for people to forget how to drive in winter weather is October 17.

The average first measurable snowfall is November 19, and the last is March 30. How late can it snow? I have a record that shows my volunteer fire department canceled their training after 11 inches of snow fell ... in mid-April.

The maximum natural temperature ever recorded was 116F, in 1936 at a place called Collegeville. You'll find that place no longer exists, as it melted, but higher unnatural temperatures have been recorded in the Statehouse during political debates.

The minimum temperature dropped to minus 36F at New Whiteland, and I don't have to tell you what made the town white that year.

In 1953, the temperature in Evansville topped 90 degrees for 105 days. Two years later, the temperature went over 100F 33 times in the same city. No one lives there anymore.

Here's one I remember well: the Blizzard of '78 (I got the t-shirt), in which a record forty inches of snow blew across northern Indiana. Another 20 inches fell in the central and south, in a storm that buried much of the country in a layer as deep as the federal deficit. It led to a federal state of emergency. (The snow, not the deficit. Well ...)

Snow way

It would be unfair to trumpet Indiana's wonderful seasons without mentioning its one un-wonderful one, winter. Actually, Indiana boasts many winter activities, including skiing, skating, maple syrup events, all sorts of Christmas festivals, and if you're really crazy, ice fishing. While my idea of winter usually matches this image along SR 8 in Albion, I'd recommend the toboggan ride at Pokagon State Park—which is refrigerated, so a lack of cold doesn't bother them anyway.

Not to be outdone, 1988 recorded the maximum ice accumulation, two inches. That led to numerous power outages and accidents, but on the brighter side there was a boon in mixed drinks. You'd go looking for ice to put in your drink too, if you got stuck with the kids for days at a time.

The highest wind gust recorded was 111 MPH, in Indianapolis. It was a hot 1929 wind ... what the heck, insert your own politician joke.

We'll cover tornados in a natural disaster segment because, despite what I said earlier, we do have our share of extreme weather. But I did find something else interesting on the subject of temperature: a high of 80, recorded in Madison in 1943, doesn't seem so bad ... except it was in January.

Compared to the minus 36 of 1994, it sounds pretty darned good.

Conversely, in 1892 the city of Marion recorded a temperature of 37—in July. In June of 1918 the temperature in La Porte got down to 30, and residents had to use ice scrapers on their horses. 1918 was a particularly bad weather year, and also the time of a terrible flu epidemic.

So, yeah, 80F? Not so bad.

Chapter Three:
YOU SAY YOU WANT A REVOLUTION?

At first glance, you might think the Revolutionary War didn't affect the future state of Indiana. It was still in the future, after all. But the French and Indian War, which kept Hoosiers from having to spell a bunch of French place names, led to the separation of the American colonies from England.

War is expensive. The English military spent a lot of resources to defend its American colonies from the French, and they felt the settlers there should be grateful enough to put up with a few taxes, just to pay off the debt from the war. Seems reasonable.

But the Americans were being taxed without representation in the English government. Also, they weren't allowed to go west, which is what America is all about. You thought it was all about prepackaged food and reality TV stars? No.

So the American colonists decided to set up their own country even though they didn't have a navy, a postal service, or even a military brass band. After all, they were only going up against the most powerful military force in the world, to do what no European colony in the history of the world had done. No problem.

Indiana was bound to get involved. Sure enough, an English army officer by the name of Henry Hamilton started paying Indians to kill the colonial settlers who'd come to the Midwest, where—granted—they weren't supposed to be.

Our story of Indiana in the Revolution starts in Kentucky, and goes to Virginia.

Haven't you ever gotten lost on a long trip?

Not That Clark—The Other One

George Rogers Clark was a surveyor, and one of the first people to venture into what would be Kentucky. When war broke out, Clark went to

Virginia, which claimed most of the lower Midwest at the time, and met with a governor by the name of Patrick Henry.

"Hey Gov, can you help me raise an army and kick Henry Hamilton's hairy hind end?"

"Oh, sure, I'll just hand over money to a surveyor with no military service, so you can leave the real fighting and wander around an Indian infested wilderness nobody cares about."

"Exactly! Thanks, Governor!"

"Okay, let's work on your sense of sarcasm."

Vigo on the Wabash

Wait—shouldn't there be a statue of George Rogers Clark at the George Rogers Clark National Historical Park? There is, but there's also this guy perched along the banks of the Wabash River. Fur trader Giuseppe Maria Francesco Vigo was also an informant, who got word to Clark when the British retook Vincennes and Fort Sackville during the Revolution.

Vigo also gave Clark money to finance the war in the Northwest, helped found what became Vincennes University, and arranged for the large bell on the Vigo County Courthouse (You can see how he might be interested in Vigo County). That seems worthy of a statue.

Clark gathered up about two hundred farmers, who brought their own rifles and knives but no uniforms—just buckskin clothes. They reached Indiana at the Falls of the Ohio, which means I've mentioned almost all the future states along the Ohio except Illinois. Then they went to Illinois.

Specifically, this untrained rabble of farmers and trappers decided to attack a fort at Kaskaskia, which at the time was on the east bank of the Mississippi River. (Now it's on the west bank, surrounded by the state of Missouri—long story.) It would, clearly, be a disaster.

They took Kaskaskia without firing a shot.

French settlers remained in the area, and they promised to support Clark if he, in turn, promised to guarantee them freedom of religion. He said "Sure—we'll work it into a constitution", and together they marched through frozen swamps back into Indiana, where they found the fort at Vincennes unoccupied.

Clark renamed it Fort Patrick Henry, possibly to guarantee the Virginia governor would keep the supplies coming. But up in Detroit Henry Hamilton heard about it, and led an army that took Vincennes-Patrick Henry back—again, without firing a shot. Hamilton renamed it yet again, so it became Fort Vincennes-Patrick Henry-Sackville.

Clark didn't like that. Patrick Henry probably wasn't thrilled, either.

But the English outnumbered him and it was in the deepest of winter. Travel was impossible, and the English would never consider coming out to fight … *hm*. A light bulb went off over Clark's head, which was odd because light bulbs hadn't been invented yet.

In February—ever tried to walk through a frozen swamp in Indiana in February? Yeah— he led 180 men though areas so flooded they had to search out shallow areas to sleep without drowning. The water got neck deep. Clark thought to rally the men by singing "Yankee Doodle" as he walked ahead, but really they wanted to catch up so they could kill him.

But eventually they made it, and marched through Vincennes (as the town was still named) to Fort Sackville. At dawn the British soldiers poked their heads above the barricades of Fort Sackville and got them shot off. The Americans brought with them a neat weapon called the Kentucky Rifle, and they knew how to use them in any state. Hamilton was captured, and as punishment lost the right to name the fort.

Today Vincennes is a (relatively) small town with a French heritage and an American identity, and not a single street or building is named after Henry Hamilton or his hairy hind end.

That one victory assured American control over the Midwest, an area almost as big as the thirteen colonies to the east. Clark could explain that easily enough:

"Great things have been affected by a few men well conducted."

A few years later more great things would happen thanks to a relative of his, who helped head up the Lewis and Clark expedition. Just to be clear, he was related to Clark, not Lewis.

Fun fact: In 1934 a memorial was built to George Rogers Clark, who boated and waded through so much water to do such great things. Within six weeks, the memorial, in Vincennes, began leaking. Well, it's a fun fact if you weren't the contractor.

George Rogers Clark National Historical Park, Vincennes

When asked where he wanted to be buried, Revolutionary War hero George Rogers Clark replied: "Why? What did you hear?" He should have said "Bury me at my national memorial, even if you have to dig me up and bury me again." Clark died in 1818 in Locust Grove, Kentucky. When later exhumed, having not reminded anyone to take him to his memorial, he was reburied near Louisville. The memorial was built at the believed site of Fort Sackville at Vincennes, which he—to coin a phrase—sacked during the Revolution. Maybe that's where the term came from.

An unusual coda to the Sackville-Vincennes adventure came on March 2nd, 1779, in the form of a reinforcement fleet that sailed to help the besieged British Sackville fort force.

Yes, I said "fleet". In the decades after, a great deal of drainage was done throughout Indiana, but at the time much of the state consisted of swamps that often flooded through the late winter and spring, leaving rivers hundreds of yards wide. So the British set out with seven boats, carrying forty soldiers, supplies, and even trade goods for the Native Americans.

Naval battle for Indiana
There's nothing really to see here, which is why I included this photo. Things were a lot swampier back then, and often flooded, so it's completely believable that the westernmost naval battle of the Revolutionary War happened here. But knowing you can stand there, turn completely around, and see absolutely no water just makes me grin.

Colonial Captain Leonard Helms, who led fifty volunteers in three boats, ambushed the British. The battle was brief (as in no one fired a shot), but it was the final nail in the floating coffin of British interests in the Wabash Valley.

(Captain Helms was probably itching for payback, as he'd been in command of Fort Sackville for a while ... during the time it was renamed Fort Patrick Henry.)

As a result you can now find, north of Vincennes in Sullivan County, an historical marker that shows the site of the westernmost naval battle of the entire Revolutionary War.

Here's the fun part: Stand by the sign and look around. There's not a pond, not a stream, not a water filled pothole (even though the sign's by a four lane highway) to be seen where this naval clash took place—depending on the time of year and the weather, of course.

From the way the marker is worded, it appears the actual battle happened on the nearby Wabash River itself, near a place called Pointe Coupee. But admitting that would spoil the irony.

Now that America had it, what was to be done with this vast area of land north of the Ohio River and east of the Mississippi? Since George Rogers Clark, the guy who kicked forts and took names, officially worked for the Virginia Militia, Virginia tried to claim the whole area.

New York, Connecticut, and Massachusetts also claimed some parts. But even back then the Feds weren't thrilled to let the states have too much stuff, and by 1800 all the land had been turned into "The Territory Northwest of the River Ohio". That name's exhausting, so we call it the Northwest Territory. Eventually it would become Indiana, Ohio, Illinois, Michigan, Wisconsin, and a bit of Minnesota, but Indiana was obviously the most important part.

We should consider ourselves lucky the original idea didn't go through after the French and Indian War: to turn the southern Great Lakes area into the colony of Charlotina.

Charlotina. This was in honor of Queen Charlotte, but still.

Luckily for us, at the time England banned colonists from the area. Without colonists, there's not much point in a colony. But the new United States government didn't recognize that ban, and the first official settlement came to Marietta, Ohio, in 1788.

The American Indians didn't like that one bit.

Some people say this marked the beginning of broken treaties and promises made by expanding Europeans to the natives. That's just silly—we broke promises long before that. From 1785-1795 members of at least a dozen tribes battled the US for control of the Northwest Territory, supported by a still smarting British Empire.

Still flush from victory over the British, the brand new American military marched into the Norwest territory, where they got their butts kicked. General Harmar was harmed; Major Hamtramck was hamstrung; Captain Armstrong was strong armed; Ensign Hartshorn was shorn of victory ... somebody stop me.

(One of the conflicts started near the site of present day Churubusco, which was named after a later American victory in the Mexican War. Churubusco's nickname is Turtle Town USA, ironically unrelated to the Chief Little Turtle who became famous for beating the Americans.)

This all led to the Battle of the Wabash, which is often called St. Clair's Defeat, which pretty much tells you who won. A thousand Indians led by Little Turtle and others whipped General Arthur—yep, St. Clair—and inflicted the biggest Indian defeat of the American army ever. Take that, General Custer.

St. Clair led a thousand men into battle, and left with twenty-four. In fact, the losses included a quarter of the entire US Army of the time.

President George Washington casted around for a new commander: someone who could defeat the Indians once and for all. His advisors said, "You'd have to be mad to take that job!"

That perked Washington up. "I know a man whose middle name is Mad!"

But Washington was mistaken: Mad was his *first* name. You have to wonder what Mad Anthony Wayne's mother was thinking, back when women in labor didn't get the good drugs.

Actually, General Wayne's fierce fighting in numerous Revolutionary War battles earned him the nickname. He became the first American General to establish a basic training program, so you have Wayne to thank for drill sergeants.

When ready, Wayne made his base of operations a place called Fort Recovery—the exact location where St. Clair was so badly defeated. Message, much? Then he led his army to the newly built Defiance, in the not yet state of Ohio. Then, finally, he met the Western Confederacy of Indians at a place called Fallen Timbers.

So I have to tell you why it was called that? Oh, okay: There had been a recent severe storm, possibly a tornado, which would be no surprise for that area. It hit along the Maumee River, not far from where Toledo, Ohio now stands, and the Indian leaders Little Turtle and Blue Jacket thought the fallen trees would slow down Wayne's five thousand men. But the American attacker was mad—*mad*, I say.

The defeated Indians retreated to Fort Miami, then controlled by their British allies even though the British were supposed to have evacuated the territory. When they knocked on the door, the British stuck their fingers in their ears and sang "La la la, we don't know where your supplies came from ..."

Being named after an Asian country isn't the only way the Indians couldn't catch a break.

24

The Battle of Fallen Timbers was such a decisive victory that it forced a treaty which kicked all the British out of the Northwest Territory, and secured it for the United States. It also led directly to Indiana's second largest city. Wayne moved on to a place called Kekionga, where he ordered the building of a fort and—after all, he just won a war—named it after himself. It was an important junction of three rivers, and the city that rose around the fort also came to be called Fort Wayne. There is no Fort Little Turtle.

Mad Anthony Wayne slept here. Well, near here.

With so much early travel done by water, the confluence of three rivers would have to be a strategically important place. Just ask the Miami Indians, whose village of Kekionga stood near where the St. Joseph, St. Marys, and Maumee rivers joined. Or Revolutionary War hero Anthony Wayne, who took it from them.

But his fort held up pretty well, didn't it? Actually, this is an exacting reproduction of the 1815 fort, the last and most sophisticated one, which stands just a short distance from the original. The first fort at the Three Rivers came in 1715, when the French built Fort Miami. The natives took it back until 1794, when Wayne came along. In 1823 the place became a settlers' village, then a city. Did I mention the Miami Indians didn't like him?

Historic Fort Wayne opened in 1976, near the nation's bicentennial, which is a pretty cool way to celebrate.

Indiana Facts:

HOOSIER DADDY?

There are two famous American nicknames, Yankee and Hoosier, with one thing in common:

Nobody knows what the heck they mean.

Oh, those aren't the only nicknames. Ohioans are called Buckeyes. "Suckers" is a name sometimes applied to the residents of Illinois; apparently it has to do with their choice in governors. Michigan is the Great Lakes State, and there's not much doubt of where that came from. Oklahoma was bound to get a nickname, Sooner or later.

But Hoosier?

The name first became common way back: a new boat built in 1831 was named the "Indiana Hoosier". It went nationwide and more in a poem called "The Hoosier's Nest". Remember, they had no TV or radio to break up the poetry. Soon it was being used a lot, even though no one knew if it was a compliment or an insult.

Historian Jacob P. Dunn, Jr. decided to track down the truth. He discovered an Anglo-Saxon word "hoo", meaning hill. Why they didn't just say hill I don't know, but apparently that turned into "hoozer", which meant anything unusually large to people in Cumberland, England. Some of those people moved to the Appalachians, where they didn't want to be called Cumberlandians. By the time they reached southern Indiana the name was set.

Or was it? After all, Indiana doesn't have large mountains, and as previously established, we're a skinny state. But then, if the phrase meant the people from Cumberland, they were likely the same size wherever they went.

There are other theories, among them:

Indiana flatboat crewmen, shipping corn to New Orleans, were called "hoosa men" after the Indian word for corn, "hoosa". This theory fails to account for the fact that the Indians never called corn "hoosa".

A contractor in Louisville, Kentucky, liked hiring workers from Indiana, who came to be called "Hoosier's Men". Eventually that was shortened to Hoosier, because we got some women.

Indiana men working on the Ohio and Mississippi Rivers developed a reputation as good fighters, and got so good at hushing up their opponents they became known as "hushers". Because alcohol was often involved, that got slurred to "Hoosiers".

Pioneer settlers in Indiana developed a habit of answering a knock on their door by calling, "Who's yere?" Why that would apply only to Indiana is beyond me, as I've heard that exact phrase, spoken that exact way, in Kentucky.

Here's my favorite: James Whitcomb Riley, a famous Indiana writer, claims Indiana men were such vicious fighters they would employ any tactics, which included biting off noses and ears. It became common for men who entered a tavern the next morning to find there'd been, shall we say, an audio bite left on the floor. This would cause them to say ... wait for it ...

Made by the most famous Hoosier Rail-Splitter himself?

Well, no. Like just about everything at Abraham Lincoln's boyhood home site, this rail fence is a reproduction. Still, it's a darn good reproduction of what things were like in the early 1800s, and he certainly had experience splitting his own rails.

"Whose ear?"

That one's the best.

Whatever the origin of the term, Indiana residents now wear the tag Hoosier, and will defend it to the death, or at least the ear. We don't care if it started out good or bad; now it's a point of pride.

Of course, we also call our favorite bean bag toss game "corn hole", so how much pride could we have?

Chapter Four:
BUT YOU GOTTA KNOW THE TERRITORY!

1800 was a great year for Indiana.

In fact, it was such a great year it got fat—well, big—and spent the next sixteen years on a diet.

Before that the place didn't exist: What we now call Indiana was part of the Northwest Territory, which as mentioned earlier included the current states of Michigan, Indiana, Ohio, Illinois, and Wisconsin, and a snowy sliver of Minnesota.

But people (that is, white people) kept coming, and by 1800 there were enough to hold an election. The people got together and said, "Let's kick Ohio out of the group!" So they did, in a case of territory divorce that dissolved the Northwest Territory. Ohio got to keep the football, and Indiana got the basketball.

Since Indiana got all the other future states, you can see who had the better lawyer. But Ohio left with, if not the last laugh, at least the first one: They became the first state carved out of Northwest Territory land, in 1803. The rest of the Northwest Territory got its name changed to ... wait for it ... the Indiana Territory.

Meanwhile, and perhaps not surprisingly, a former Indian fighter was appointed congressman to represent that Indiana Territory. He was William Henry Harrison, and early on he realized the new state needed more people, just in case they ever established a statewide sporting system. He convinced Congress to lower the price of land in the territory, and allowed newcomers to get the land on credit, and pay for it later. Thus his nickname, "MasterCard Harrison".

The rush was on.

Soon President John Adams named Harrison the first Indiana Territory Governor. He moved to a place called Grouseland (I'm not making that up) in the territory's new capital, Vincennes.

You might recall Vincennes as a small French village—inhabited by French, not moved here from France. It was fought over so many times its fort ended up called Fort Vincennes-Patrick Henry-Sackville, which would be something for the inhabitants to Grouse over. In a way the location's a little odd: too far southeast to be near the center of the vast Indiana territory, but not close to where almost all the people lived, along the Ohio River. Today it's about halfway between Indianapolis and St. Louis, assuming you go out of your way a little to see the Grouseland museum.

Eventually the Indiana Territory shed its excess weight, losing Michigan in 1805 and the western tier of other future states in 1809. Soon it was its current shape—slim, trim, and ready for racing.

But first there was the matter of a little war to consider.

Prophet and Loss

William Henry Harrison tried to buy most of the Indiana Indian lands from Indiana Indians, but as the old saying goes when it comes to treaties, treaters never prosper. Not only did the Indians not get their money, but there was some dispute about whether individual tribes had the right to sell certain lands.

Soon a new leader stepped forward, a Shawnee named Tecumseh who'd fought at Fallen Timbers. He and his brother, a medicine man called The Prophet, banded the tribes together into what they hoped would be a new nation. It helped that The Prophet once predicted the disappearance of the sun at midday, without mentioning he'd heard about an eclipse from a Canadian trader.

You can't buy magic like that.

Tecumseh's men readied for a fight, especially after The Prophet explained his magic would keep bullets from hitting them. When Tecumseh left for a speaking tour in 1811 (yeah, a speaking tour), he told The Prophet to keep it down and not bother the neighbors until he returned.

But The Prophet threw a huge party, and invited all his friends.

Harrison, a hands-on governor, led an army to what became the Battle of Tippecanoe in which, to my knowledge, no canoes were tipped at all. The Prophet attacked first, and turned out to be a little off on the magic thing. He also didn't cast any protective spells over their town, which afterward no longer existed. To add insult to bullet holes, The Prophet apparently forgot about Harrison being an experienced Indian fighter.

Tecumseh got back, saw the police had been called to break up the party, and said "We just can't have anything nice!" Then he moved to Canada, where at least the British appreciated him. The town where the battle happened is now known as Battleground, and it's right next to Prophetstown State Park.

Unfortunately, in December of 1811 a giant earthquake centered on New Madrid, Missouri, rocked and rolled the entire Midwest and beyond. Shaken Indians took it as a sign they should support Tecumseh, so instead of dropping, Indian attacks increased. Tecumseh's federation of area tribes would join the British to war against the Americans the very next year, apparently forgetting how badly that went for them before.

And Harrison? We'll hear more about him.

When was the War of 1812?

Or: Yeah, and who's buried in Grant's Tomb?

The English, sore losers after the Revolution, encouraged Indian attacks on American settlers. Meanwhile, the British military had a lot of resources tied up in Europe, fighting this guy Napoleon something-or-other. Short on manpower, they began to stop American ships and force American sailors into the British Navy. It was called impressment, and no one was impressed.

As a result, in 1812 the unimaginatively named War of 1812 broke out. (Technically it was the War of 1812-14, but that doesn't roll off the tongue so well.) A lot of people think the war took place along the coastlines, what with the burning of Washington, the shelling of Fort McHenry, and the Battle of New Orleans.

But US troops headed north, intend on invading Canada—as if they'd ever done anything to us. Led by generals who weren't necessarily general material, the US soldiers got a cold reception. If they'd won, the Canadian provinces might today be part of the United States, and we wouldn't be making jokes about them being "America's hat".

Then Indiana would be in the middle of America, instead of in the north, and we'd have to stop complaining about being so cold. "You think *you're* cold? Come visit us in the great state of Manitoba, eh?"

Instead, British and Canadian soldiers tromped every attempt at invasion and even occupied eastern Maine, where from a weather viewpoint they felt right at home.

Then William Henry Harrison said, "I'm back in the game!" He left the governor's position and led an army against the English in Canada.

Getting to Canada proved difficult, since the British army occupied Detroit. Americans took it in the summer of 1812, after American General William Hull went to Canada to get a Sandwich—that is, the town of Sandwich, now part of Windsor. Taking exception to his luncheon plans, Tecumseh joined British and Canadian troops to not only beat Hull, but follow him back to the states and reconquer Detroit.

That gave them control of most of Michigan and the Great Lakes. Joined by Tecumseh's warriors, the British attacked Fort Wayne and other communities, under the theory it was way too cold in Canada to give up their Great Lakes bases.

In October the Americans tried again, this time headed for Niagara, but the honeymoon was over—they were beaten then, and again in 1813 when they failed to capture Montreal.

The embattled soldiers were saved by ... sailors. In late 1813, after a fast season of ship building, America Admiral Oliver Hazard Perry beat up the British navy on the Great Lakes. Now Harrison could attack Detroit.

Take that, ya Limeys!
Reenactors fire a War of 1812 era cannon during the Stone's Trace Festival in Noble County. The Indiana Territory was hotly contested during the war, usually by small groups of Americans taking on combined English and Native American forces. When cannon were used at all, they were usually smaller pieces like this, which could be more easily transported through the wilderness.

Harrison arrived to discover Detroit to be, much like today, largely abandoned. Not to be deterred, Harrison chased the British all the way to the Thames River.

No, not the Thames that goes through London: the one in Canada, where in October, 1813, Harrison caught up with the retreating British forces. He killed or captured every British soldier and killed Tecumseh, too. Not Harrison personally; his army did a lot of it.

As a result, America secured control over the Northwest Territory, with only a few skirmishes later on. The Battle of the Thames pretty much ended the War of 1812 as far as Indiana was concerned, which was a good thing: They had only a few years to prepare for statehood.

Indiana Facts:
STATE SYMBOLS PART 1, OR: CRY ME A RIVER

This may be the single most important section about Indiana facts you'll ever read. After all, if you don't know the state symbols, how can you brag about them in, say, Nebraska? How will you hold your own in a symbol slam in Hoboken? I rest my case.

Some of them are well known, such as the state bird.

It's the *cardinal*. Sheesh.

I should add St. Louis stole the cardinal from Indiana, not the other way around. If Indiana had a big league pro baseball team, I assure you it would be the Cardinals. Come to think of it, it should probably be the Hoosiers. Never mind.

The male cardinal is bright red, which is from where Roman Catholic Cardinals get their clothing color. Most people don't know the favorite sport of Cardinals in the Church is not baseball—those thieving St. Louis people—but basketball, which is why religious people tend to be tall. Now, basketball is the unofficial Indiana sport, and Cardinals love basketball, and our state bird is the cardinal, so there you go.

The state river is the Wabash, which doesn't seem all that obvious at first. But the Wabash River, which runs 411 miles to the Ohio, is the longest free-flowing river east of the Mississippi. Take that, Delaware! (The river, not the state. Or the tribe.)

The Wabash is actually 503 miles long, starting in northwest Ohio before it becomes the largest northern tributary to the Ohio River. A dam near Huntington cuts off the first 90 miles or so, which is why only 411 miles of it is "free-flowing" ... but that's mostly Ohio, so who cares?

The Muddy Wabash

An angry Wabash River flows through a normally calm area of Huntington County. Runoff from 2015 flooding swelled the river beyond its banks, and turned it a muddy brown, just so Mother Nature could remind humans who's really in charge.

The river became so popular that a county each in Indiana and Illinois, eight townships, a city, town, two colleges, canal, and four warships are named after it. Those ships include a frigate, a freighter, and two oilers—an oiler being a supply ship that carries coal. Or is it wood?

Taking all this into consideration, it's no surprise the state song is "On the Banks of the Wabash, Far Away". With a river that long, you can be on the banks and still be far away from the rest of it.

The song was written by Paul Dresser of Terre Haute, and first published in 1897. Just as Francis Scott Key waited many years before his poem, "The Star Spangled Banner", made it to National Anthem status, Dresser also had to wait. He didn't have to sit through a battle, though.

Despite the length of its title, "On the Banks of the Wabash, Far Away" was one of the bestselling songs of the 19th century. The song was all about Dresser's childhood life, which took place near pretty much where you think it did, and it earned over a hundred thousand dollars from the sale of sheet music. (MTV was unable to make use of the song for video, as TV had not yet been invented and that left only M.)

In 1913 the General Assembly made it Indiana's state song, and in 1923 it was even turned into a movie with the same title. As often happens in movies, it was a loose adaptation. Also loosely adapted were versions that included an 1898 anti-war song and another that turned into a number one hit—in Sweden.

You may not remember *that* song so much, but if you've ever watched the Indianapolis 500 you probably know of a song that borrowed so heavily from Dreiser's work many are convinced to this day it's blatant plagiarism. But that song has a catchier title: "Back Home Again In Indiana".

By the way, there was another famous Dresser at the time: Paul's brother Theodore, one of Indiana's most famous novelists, who once claimed to have written some of the song's lyrics. Dresser didn't get much public support, as he was an open communist and professed a dislike of … Indiana.

You may think this discussion of river songs is for the birds, but we'll continue to talk about Indiana symbols and emblems in a future segment.

Chapter Five:

SAY, THIS LOOKS LIKE A GOOD PLACE FOR A STATE

Harrison retired from public service in 1813, not even bothering to wait for Andrew Jackson to clean things up at The Battle of New Orleans. Harrison retired to North Bend, Ohio, never to be in the public eye again. (Heh.) Interestingly, North Bend is substantially south of South Bend.

John Gibson had taken over as acting Governor while Harrison rode out to do warrior stuff, and later President Madison appointed Thomas Posey to the post. Meanwhile the territorial capital was moved from the almost-central Vincennes to the way-not-central-at-all Corydon, along the Ohio River. This guaranteed Vincennes would fade away, while Corydon would become a huge, bustling metropolis.

The whole question of the territorial government would become a moot point, which is like a woot point, but without the excitement.

Hoosiers petitioned the US Congress to make Indiana a state in 1812, but as it happened other events of interest went on at the time. Also, it's Congress—surely no one expected them to make a decision right away. But in early 1816 a census revealed an astounding 63,897 people in Indiana—where did they put them all?—which put the population above the statehood threshold.

I didn't even know they made excavators back then

Indiana's first capitol building, in Corydon, is seen here along with a circa 1816 excavator. Or, possibly, it was a more modern excavator being used in restoration work on the capital square. Construction on the building began in 1814, using good old fashioned Indiana limestone, and cost $1,500. The excavator was made of plain old steel. After the capital was moved to Indianapolis it was used as a county courthouse, until the state bought it back in 1917. I mean the building was, not the excavator.

It all went quickly after that, with a constitutional convention in 1816 that produced, indeed, a constitution. Elections came in August, just weeks after election fatigue arrived, and on December 11, 1816, President Madison approved Indiana's admission as the 19th United State.

Yay!

That "retired" guy you might remember, William Henry Harrison, was later elected a U.S. Representative and Senator ... from Ohio. It turns out that while Indiana has South Bend, he still preferred North Bend.

But that's okay, because Indiana had its own governor—its very first state governor. So there, Senator Harrison.

Jinkies, Jennings!

Let's go back a bit. What, you've got some place to be? It's all well and good to be governor of the Indiana territory, but the real action was to be governor of a state. It's kind of like the first President of the United States *before* the Constitution—there was one, but does anyone remember who? No, they just remember George Washington galloping in to save the day after the Constitution was ratified.

By the way, the first President under the Articles of Confederation was John Hanson. He was technically President of the Continental Congress. Maybe it's ironic that he was responsible for the first southern troops sent to join George Washington during the Revolution. And, of course, it was Washington who later sent Mad Anthony Wayne to secure Indiana for the U.S.

It's a six degree thing.

But never mind Hanson, he's just an example. Poor Hanson. No, I want to talk about Jonathan Jennings, who came down the Ohio River on a flatboat to be a lawyer and newspaper publisher in the Indiana Territory.

Lawyer? There goes the territory.

Jennings was an energetic guy and hit the road—or, more likely, the trails—to shake hands and get elected to Congress in 1809. He got reelected in 1811 and petitioned for statehood (for Indiana, not himself). Then the War of 1812 came along, to disrupt pretty much everyone's plans.

But Jennings had little else to do, as cable TV didn't reach the frontier until after the Civil War, so he petitioned again in 1816. This time it flew, and he got to be president of the state constitution convention. Forty-three delegates crammed into the Harrison County Courthouse (remember Harrison?). It was cramped and hot and the air conditioner repairman couldn't make it from Maryland, so the delegates took to meeting outside, under a giant elm tree in Corydon.

The Constitutional Elm passed away in 1925 of Dutch elm disease, and you have to wonder if the Dutch were just jealous of our system of government. Today the Indiana Constitution is displayed in the Statehouse, in a wood case made from that elm, which is probably not what the elm would have preferred. Meanwhile the Constitutional Elm's trunk is preserved inside a brick encasement, which stands in someone's front yard in an otherwise quiet Corydon neighborhood. So far as I know, Jennings isn't preserved at all.

Under Jennings' leadership, the Indiana Constitution created a three part state government: a General Assembly, a State Governor, and a Supreme Court.

Say, I think he stole that from somewhere.

The Constitutional Elm, Corydon

The Constitutional Elm still stood proud in Corydon when the centennial of Indiana's first constitution was celebrated, in 1916. By 1925 it had died thanks to the Dutch, who, jealous of the state's system of government, gave the elm a disease. The trunk is now preserved, at the spot where overheated legislatures gathered under its shade. The new constitutional was the first in the country to ban slaves, and mandate funding for public schools.

The trunk was preserved with coal tar, so ... it's really seen better days. As the bicentennial approached efforts were underway to restore it, and the Dutch have been banned from the state.

After several fist fights and sword duels, the delegates voted to ban slavery in Indiana, which was cool. Only white men could vote, which was not so cool, but in line with the rest of the country. They also made Indiana the first state to have a state-funded public school system, which brings us back to cool, and set aside a township for a public university. That location in Bloomington would later be invaded by rabid basketball fans and became Indiana University.

The last big job was to appoint a state governor. Did I mention Jonathan Jennings? He was in charge when Indiana became the nineteenth state on December 11, 1816.

What? No Gymnasium?

A good example of Indiana's early one room schools still stands in northwest Noble County. The schools were placed to be within walking distance of most students, and featured such luxuries as a pot-bellied stove, outhouse, and a nice, sturdy hickory switch.

Go West, Young—Oh, Hi

Becoming a state is a lot like drinking a six pack of beer: It'll open the floodgates. They came on flatboats, they came in wagons, they came in coach class on the *Titanic* ... well, that last group never quite got here.

Individuals came, and large groups. Just before statehood, a man named George Rapp led a group of 800 people on flatboats to the banks of the Wabash River, where Rapp intended to start a utopian society.

That kind of stuff gets a bad Rapp these days.

By all accounts the members of this group were hard workers who cleared the land, drained swamps, and began farming around a town they called Harmonie. That's Harmonie, not Hermione—you Harry Potter fans settle down. They put their blood and sweat into brick buildings, a church, a sawmill, groves of fruit trees, and more mobile groves of livestock.

Within twenty years the people said, "What—this is a utopia?" and moved back to Pennsylvania. This is a not uncommon fate for utopian societies, especially ones that can't spell harmony.

Still, the land was bought up by a guy named Robert Owen, who imaginatively named it New Harmony. Under the correct spelling, the town attracted a thousand teachers and scholars to what Owen hoped to be a model community. But, hit by a shortage of modeling glue, Owen was forced to give up.

So why mention this place, specifically? Because giving up isn't what Hoosiers do. Most of this new group stayed, and to this day New Harmony exists on the backs of Owen and Rapp, and I don't mean that literally because they're buried elsewhere. New Harmony, once cutting edge, is now a beautiful historic town of antiques, art galleries, and architecture.

What would the government be without offices?

Right next to the first state capitol building in Corydon stands the first state office building, because, hey—bureaucracy. In 2015 both buildings underwent upgrades to, among other things, keep water out and electricity in.

Indiana Facts:
STATE SYMBOLS PART 2, OR: MORE INTO INDY

We covered birds, rivers, and songs, but no discussion of Indiana would be complete without flags, plants, and pie.

Pie?

It might be hard to see the necessity, but the Indiana Senate struggled over the critical issues of the state pie and the state beverage. In 2007, after decades of debate that included threats, filibusters, and stick fights on the Senate floor, that august body decided on:

Sugar cream pie.

Yum.

Why? Well, not only did the Senators need something to campaign on that year, but sugar cream pie is also known as Hoosier Pie, a tradition that dates back to early movers and shakers such as Amish and ... Shakers. (They shook. Long story.)

Perhaps they shook from too much sugar, back in the 1800s when diabetes blood tests were not yet available. Still, whether you call it sugar cream or Hoosier, whether it results in a feeling of fullness and satisfaction or a lifelong medical condition—it's just good.

Oh, and the state beverage? Well, the Senate must have given up on that one, because they chose ...

Water.

Hopefully it was at least water from the Wabash River.

Let's take a look at still more signs and symptoms of symbols and emblems:

State Poem: "Indiana", by Arthur Franklin Mapes.

This is a favorite of mine, as Mapes was a native to my home county, and I had help from a relative of his on a previous book project. Besides, you can't beat the title. Mapes was a machinist at Flint and Walling

Manufacturing, a company that shipped pumps and windmills across the world. His poems are more homebodies. "Indiana" in particular hits on all the great stuff: hills, lakes, woods, streams, rail fences and sycamores, and the Wabash River. If there's a paradise on Earth, he describes it.

State Rifle: The Grouseland rifle.

It was the gun that opened up Indiana to settlers, along with the plow, the sugar cream pie, and the treaty with disappearing ink. Still, the Grouseland?

Turns out it's the most Hoosier of guns. Named after the home of William Henry Harrison (remember him?) in Vincennes, it was designed by John Small. Forget his name: He was a big man, who designed the state seal and served as Indiana's first sheriff (of Knox County.)

Small was also a captain of the local militia, a tavern owner, and a legislator in the Indiana Territory ... oh, and the county he was sheriff of, Knox, at the time took up much of Indiana, Illinois, Wisconsin, and Michigan.

Small was a big man.

State language: English.

You'd think that would be a given.

State flower: Peony.

Believe it or not, there was an ongoing fight over the state flower. Yeah. In 1913 the General Assembly adopted the carnation, until someone pointed out the carnation wasn't native to Indiana. Oops.

Instead, after ten years of having that pointed out, the tulip tree blossom was chosen. Why not have that be the state tree? Well, in 1931, among rumors that a Hoosier zinnia seed farmer stuck his flowery hand into the debate, the zinnia was adopted. In 1957 the General Assembly was about to pick the dogwood, but as it happened one of the state representatives at the time was a commercial peony farmer. Guess what won?

There was some familiar criticism as a result of that ... it turns out the peony was not native to Indiana. But, sensing how ridiculous the whole conflict had become, the Assembly refused to go back to the flowery drawing board, and we've been red, pink, and white ever since.

Oh, and *state tree*? Tulip tree. Apparently a consolation prize.

State aircraft: The Republic Aviation P-47 Thunderbolt.

I know, right? But it's the only World War II plane made in Indiana, in an Evansville factory. As of a few years ago, about half a dozen of them could still fly—over seventy years later.

Indiana State Nickname: This one will stun you: "The Hoosier State".

Indiana State Motto: Come on … say it with me … "The Crossroads of America".

We've reached the end of our time, which is silly because I'm the one who gets to set the end of our time. But we can't rush because later we need to explore, among other things, one of the most important symbols of any state. No, not the state stone: the state flag.

Okay, and the stone, too.

Shouldn't this be Indiana's official state barn?

At one time Indiana had more round barns than any other state, with well over a dozen in Fulton County alone. Why round? Why not? This one, in Elkhart County, is now the Amish Acres Round Barn Theater in Elkhart County. This area of northeast Indiana boasts the third-largest Amish settlement in the country.

Chapter Six:
A CAPITAL IDEA

Egypt would be jealous of this obelisk
The Indiana World War Memorial Plaza actually takes up six city blocks in downtown Indianapolis, if you include the state and national headquarters for the American Legion. That includes 24 acres of statues, monuments, fountains, sculptures, two museums, and three parks.
And this: the Veterans Memorial Plaza, which for understandable reasons is often called Obelisk Square. The 100 foot obelisk is of black granite, and the plaza has become a popular gathering place for both informal and formal groups.

When Indiana became a state in 1816 the capital, Corydon, was along the Ohio River, at the southern end. That was okay, because the center of population was also along the Ohio River, unless you were an American Indian. Central Indiana remained a wilderness, and northern Indiana was just too darned cold.

It's *still* too cold.

But it's the nature of some people to be always on the move, and move they did. The East Coast? Too crowded. Ohio? Too fat. Indiana was a nice, shapely state. (I'm talking about the states themselves—you can argue amongst yourselves about the people.)

The population worked its way north, on the hunt for land and opportunity and a nice beach, and it wasn't long before state leaders realized that they also needed to pack up and move north.

Hoosiers tended to be a common sense people, so they looked around for land close to the center of the state, and found a swampy area called Fall Creek. In

1819 a man named George Pogue built a log cabin nearby, along a creek he rather egotistically named Pogue's Run. I'm not sure you'd want to drink the water in a place with "Run" in the title.

One wonders whether Fall Creek and Pogue's Run were the same piece of water. If so, Pogue should have left it alone. Maybe he tripped and fell there, and thought the original name was mocking him. (Actually, by some accounts the creek wasn't named after Pogue until after he disappeared in 1821, in which case it becomes an ironic name.) You'll hear more about Pogue's Run, which flowed through the original plat of Indianapolis, when the Civil War comes along. In any case, most of Pogue's Run now lies *under* Indianapolis, and its path runs beneath Lucas Oil Stadium.

A few years later John Wesley McCormick also built a cabin, right in the middle of what's now called White River State Park. Never mind that it's illegal to build a home in a state park. With only two fur traders settled in the area, it wasn't hard to grab up the land for a state capital.

Well, sure, they had to kick the natives out first. This they did in 1818, signing a treaty with the Delaware Nation that required the Delaware to leave central Indiana by 1821. Pogue apparently jumped the gun ... one way or another, you know there was a gun involved.

The Delaware were experienced travelers, having originally lived along a River in New York and New Jersey called the Delaware. By leaving they missed the whole Washington's crossing party, but what can you do? The Delaware got treatied right out of the Colonies and into Ohio before they settled in Indiana. Then Missouri. Then Kansas. Now the Delaware Tribe is headquartered in Oklahoma, and you have to think they're a little tired of packing.

Their movement paved the way for a lot of paving. The capital committee had their new permanent site, which this time really was permanent, assuming the capital doesn't someday move to Terra Haute.

Why the location was two miles northwest of the geographical center instead of right on it is a mystery, but they probably wanted to avoid swampland. Besides, in the 21st century the whole area is Indianapolis, anyway, including Pogue's Run and McCormick's former homestead in White River State Park. Don't confuse that with McCormick's Creek State Park, which is further southwest and named after—John McCormick. Turns out there were two John McCormicks who lived a few dozen miles from each other—either that or one really got around by the standards of the day. There might be some irony in the fact that the Delaware used to live in both places. They should probably feel the same way about the (father and son) team of John McCormick that my part-Cherokee wife feels about Andrew Jackson.

Having chosen a location, state planners looked around for someone to design their brand new city. They settled on Alexander Ralston and Elias Pym Fordham (no, you won't be tested on the names). Ralston had some pedigree; He was the apprentice to a guy named Pierre L'Enfant, and helped L'Enfant plan another capital: Washington, D.C.

However, they didn't think much ahead: the Indiana capital they planned would be only one square mile, centered on a Governor's Circle where the executive mansion would stand. As if any government could limit itself to one square mile. (Pogue's Run ran through a corner of this area.)

The governor's house was indeed built in 1827—all ready for the governor, his family, his servants, the dog, and in those days probably sheep to keep the lawn mown, and horses for transport and fertilizer. It was a grand place, to be the center of a grand city.

No governor ever lived there.

The place was right in the middle of the town's main square—well, circle—and buzzed with so much activity that there was no privacy to speak of. The building would be used for a variety of events, none related to the governor's servants shoveling horse stalls to fertilize the lawn for the sheep. Eventually the building was torn down and replaced by a park, which is now Monument Circle: the location of the Indiana State Soldiers and Sailors Monument, the first in the nation dedicated to the "common" soldier and sailor. (Inside the base is the Colonel Eli Lilly Civil War Museum.) Legally, no building in Indianapolis can be taller than that monument, which is okay because at 284 feet it's a very tall obelisk, indeed.

It's pretty cool.

As for the governor's residence, they hauled in a double-wide trailer on the bad side of town, between the swamp and Pogue's Run. It's said sometimes, if you listen late at night, you can still hear Pogue running.

What to name the new city? "Polis" is simply Greek for "city", which made the new capital the "city of Indiana"—Indianapolis. Sometimes simplest is best.

Technically the residents of the city are called Indianapolitans, which isn't so simple at all, and it's doubtful any of them use the term. But that's up to them, and there are a lot of them: it's now the 12th largest city in the United States, and the 33rd largest metropolitan area. Anyone trying to drive around the place can confirm that.

During the Civil War Indianapolis became home to a training facility and a major prison-of-war camp, and with all the railroads coming through it made an equally major supply and support area for the Union. The Confederates even put some thought into attacking the city, although they only made it as far as Seymour, about fifty miles north of Louisville KY. A few years later Seymour was the site of the world's first moving train robbery, which led to the end of the Reno Gang at a place called Hangman's Crossing. (You can guess what that ending entailed.) Seymour wasn't renowned for its good luck in the 1860s.

It wasn't the capital's only brush with world history. In 1968, the day Martin Luther King Jr. was assassinated, Robert F. Kennedy

State Soldiers and Sailors Monument ... well, part of it

Whatever neoclassical is, it's pretty cool. Monument Circle is dead-center of downtown Indianapolis, and in the center of that is the first monument in the country dedicated to the common soldier. It stands 284 feet high, so ignore the photographer (me) cutting off the top. It was built of limestone straight from Owen County, and in its basement contains the Colonel Eli Lilly Civil War Museum—he of pharmaceutical fame. In 1902 it cost almost $600,000; replacing it would cost a cool half billion.

This is the very spot where the first governor's residence was built. If it was as busy then as it is now, it's no wonder the governor never lived there.

happened to be in town. He gave an off-the-cuff speech on race to a mostly black crowd in the inner city, which may have spared Indianapolis from the rioting that broke out in America's other major cities.

What's in a Nickname?

Contrary to popular opinion, Indianapolis' nickname is *not* "Gentlemen, Start Your Engines". In fact, the Indianapolis Motor Speedway, and thus the Indianapolis 500, is not in Indianapolis at all: It's in the adjoining town of Speedway, Indiana. See what they did, there?

But the nickname of the state capital—and officially, the whole state—is transportation related: "The Crossroads of America".

This is a fun fact, when you consider the center of Indiana was once about as inaccessible as you could get. There was a reason so many Hoosiers first settled along the Ohio River, then along the Wabash and near Lake Michigan. It was a boater's paradise, but in a transportation rather than recreation way.

In case you didn't already know
They take their motto seriously in the Corydon area, decorating hotel rooms with it. On the up side, if you wake up disoriented you'll at least be able to narrow your location down to one fiftieth of the country.

But by 1829 the National Road, also called the Cumberland Road, reached Indianapolis,

and hey—*national* road, the first one ever. Before you knew it, because you weren't born yet, roads, canals, and railroads crisscrossed the capital both over and underground. The nation's center of population reached Indiana, and in 1831 a steamboat even managed to reach Indy from the Ohio River. Unfortunately, it ran aground on the return trip, at which point people realized the White River was no Ohio.

Today you can find five interstate highways charging into the metropolitan area to meet at the Indianapolis beltway, also known as Interstate 465, otherwise known as the place cars go to disappear forever.

Locals speak in hushed tones of people who hit an onramp onto I-465 and never got off, and entire families in vans and station wagons who died of old age while trying to find their way around.

Terre Haute and Vandalia, Ohio, have also claimed the Crossroads of America title, but Indianapolis beat them up and took their candy. Figuratively speaking.

It helps that Indianapolis also served as a major hub of railroad and other traffic, as we'll see later. It's also the seat of Marion County, as if it didn't have enough to do.

He must have been a good guy

A wife would know. Emma Depew thought enough of her husband, Dr. Richard J. Depew, to bequeath $50,000 toward a fountain in his honor—and that was in 1913 money. The result is in University Park on the Veterans Memorial Plaza, which was completed in 1919. It depicts a bronze figure of a woman dancing, surrounded by eight dancing children, along with fish that, I presume, are also dancing.

Indiana Facts:
STATE SYMBOLS PART 3, OR: FLAG FLYING STONED

Let's take a quick look at some other symbols and emblems of Indiana, including the most important of all: the state flag.

(This might be argued by those who prefer the state pie.)

This book, if all goes well, will be published during Indiana's bicentennial. It's quite literally impossible to have a bicentennial without a centennial, and sure enough, in 1916 Indiana celebrated its 100th birthday. ("Centennial" is Latin for "really old". "Bicentennial" is Latin for "really old but still swinging both ways".)

The Daughters of the American Revolution sponsored a contest during the Centennial, and the winner of the contest would get a hundred bucks and be able to say they ran their idea up the flagpole, and it waved.

Out of two hundred entries, the General Assembly accepted one by Paul Hadley, an artist from Mooresville:

On a blue field, it has a gold torch to symbolize liberty and enlightenment, or possibly that the weather iced up and the power's out again. On the outer circle are thirteen stars, to symbolize the original thirteen states, and on the inner circle another five to show the next five states to join the Union. Then comes one large star above the torch, and just in case you aren't sure what it symbolizes, the name "Indiana" is right above it.

The word was not part of Hadley's original design ... perhaps he thought it was too obvious. But putting the state's name on turned out to be a brilliant concept, guaranteeing no other state would steal Indiana's flag. However, it only worked for states: In the 1992 movie *Batman Returns*, the Gotham City flag can be seen—and it looks awfully familiar.

Some brave souls talked of sneaking into Gotham to steal our flag back but ... you know ... Batman.

There's also the state seal, which is unusual because we're nowhere near the ocean. No, I mean the one that goes on the podium so no one can see if the governor's fly is open. It's a perfect circle (the seal, not the fly), crowded with a woodsman, buffalo, sycamore trees, hills, and a setting sun.

Or maybe it's a rising sun? There's been disagreement over that, and since the seal first appeared in 1801, nobody's around who remembers. That seal, for the territory rather than the state, looked a little different at the time; for instance, the woodsman was tin, and the buffalo was a cowardly lion. Or maybe the buffalo was a bison, but let's not get technical.

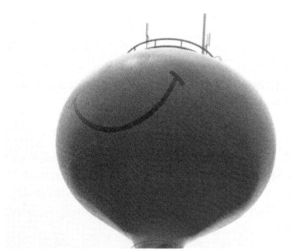

Happiness is a warm water tower

And why couldn't this be the state smile? The water tower in Ashley sports a happy face complete with bow tie, because bow ties are cool. And why is the happy face happy? Maybe it's well hydrated. It's far from the only happy faced water tower in the country, but I maintain it's the happiest.

When the seal was made official for the state in 1816 lawmakers specified the sun as setting, which seems a little strange for a dawning state. In any case it took about a century to standardize where all the symbols should stand in relation to each other, and you can imagine how nervous the buffalo got whenever the woodsman turned toward him. Maybe that's why the buffalo was always fleeing.

It wasn't until around 1918 that someone pointed out the sun seemed to set behind a mountain ... and, since the closest mountains to Indiana were to the east, the sun must actually be rising. Since then there have been at least two attempts to change the official description of the sun from "setting" to "rising".

We pay our elected officials for this stuff.

Here's a more unusual category: the state stone.

The choice? Simple: Salem Limestone. Found in south central Indiana, it's the highest quality limestone in the country. Limestone is a deposit of marine fossils—Indiana used to be great oceanfront property. Actually, it used to be the ocean. Settlers first started quarrying limestone in 1827, and in no time at all it got around: It's in Indiana's State Capitol building, buildings at Indiana University, most of the state's courthouses, monuments all over ... but that's not all.

Look for Indiana limestone in the Empire State Building, the Pentagon, Yankee Stadium, 35 of 50 state capitol buildings, the original Rockefeller Center, Hotel Macdonald in Edmonton, Canada ... let me take a breath ... well, the list goes on. After the Great Chicago Fire, Chicagoans, a bit leery of wood construction, used Indiana limestone extensively.

It's good stuff, and the most commonly used building stone in the nation. All from little sea animals in an ocean that no longer exists.

I'm Not Lion

Shield-bearing limestone lions—Indiana limestone, natch—guard the north and south entrances of the Indiana World War Memorial Building in Indianapolis. There are, without a doubt, many priceless artifacts in the building's museum ... but even Lara Croft wouldn't mess with these guys.

Chapter Seven:
YOU *CAN* GET THERE FROM HERE

As you saw earlier, we were going to talk about transportation in more detail later. It's later.

Yes, Indianapolis, and by extension Indiana, became the Crossroads of America, but how it go there was a bit ... well, meandering. Yes, it's true Indianapolis was reached by the east-west National Highway, the first one of its kind, which came along a century before the interstate highway system. But it didn't reach Indianapolis until a decade after the city itself came along. After all, it had to make its way across Ohio and Pennsylvania, and they're fat.

(Portly? Slim challenged?)

One of the reasons Indianapolis sprang up where it did—and this explains it being two miles northwest of the state's actual center—was the White River. Back in those days, the best way to reach anything was by water, so having the city on a waterway seemed vitally important. Paddleboats! Riverboats! Bikini ladies on jet skis!

Best of all, most Indiana rivers flowed to the Ohio River, and thus the Mississippi, and thus New Orleans. In theory someone could set out from Indianapolis on the White River and end up partying at Mardi Gras, without setting foot off their boat.

This might be a good time to point out that, so far as I know, the White River was not racially named. It just sometimes looks white. I don't know why ... drowning mimes? On the other hand, the state government kicked out most of the Indians and, despite declaring Indiana to be slave-free, passed a law that denied entrance to freed blacks. Maybe I should double check the naming process.

Nobody thought to make sure the river ran deep enough for big boats. It didn't. Remember, one paddleboat did indeed make it to Indy, but bottomed out and almost didn't make it back. Sailors hate that kind of stuff.

But did the state leaders despair and turn on the waterworks? Well yeah, kind of. Still fixated on water transportation, they came up with a clear solution: Canals! It worked on Mars, didn't it?

Author's note: It didn't work on Mars, despite what Percival Lovell thought. Apparently he took too many trips to the Mars bar. There are no canals on Mars—update your encyclopedia.

The Indiana General Assembly came up with a mammoth idea, possibly the most mammoth idea since the mammoth: a system of canals would crisscross the area, bringing to every corner of the state supplies, people, trade, and dancing girls. (This might be a good time to point out that women didn't have the vote yet.)

They named the project the Mammoth Improvement Act. See? Mammoth.

But the state was only twenty years old; how would it pay for such a project? I know—take out loans! What could possibly go wrong? Governments don't go uncontrollably into debt. If there's too much red ink, we'll dump it in the White River and change the name.

So that's what they did. The loans, I mean—the Red River is down in Texas.

You'd think they would have learned their lesson from the nationwide Panic of 1819, which led to the country's very first depression. In their defense, only two Indiana banks got bankrupted by that economic downturn. On the other hand, at the time there were only two Indiana banks. Thank goodness an economic crash would never happen again.

Eight major infrastructure projects were part of the Mammoth Improvement Act, and as you might imagine they were all major—one might even say mammoth. One canal would run for almost three hundred miles: It would start at Logansport, where there would be a port, and then through Indianapolis to Evansville, where there would be a ville. The plan would eventually connect Lake Erie in the northeast with the Ohio River in the south, which would be very mammoth, indeed. And I don't use "very" very often.

Feverish work began across the state. (It was cold and flu season.) Much of the canal building involved building canals, but not all: Dams were also put up to provide reservoirs to keep the canals filled. Being a government operation, money probably also went to items such as overhead, paper-pushing, and the General Assembly Committee to Recruit Dancing Girls. The dancing girl plan disintegrated in 1849, when all the girls headed west for the Forty-Niner gold fields and related saloons.

Actually, the whole plan crashed and burned. Four years after the Mammoth Improvement Act passed, the entire state went mammothly bankrupt and all work stopped. For a while a horse-drawn barge brought goods to Indianapolis, but then all the horses drowned. Two dozen miles of canal were finished near Indianapolis, but only a little over eight miles ever saw use as they took goods and passengers from the city north to Broad Ripple. That made the only ripple in the once great transportation plan, and it wasn't really that broad. Who names these towns?

Still, to this day some remnants of the massive—excuse me, mammoth—project remain. Part of the Central Canal can be seen in White River State Park, along with the river, which still runs white. No mime bodies were ever found.

In my own home county, Noble, one of the huge reservoirs still remains: Now called Sylvan Lake, it's become a major recreational area. Not far from it, a short section of road follows the remains of the feeder canal. If you ever find yourself driving down a Canal Road in Indiana, you can bet you're following history. Remember, don't drive into water. You're not a boat.

The Colossus of Roads

It's no wonder everyone wanted to go by boat, considering the terrible condition of the roads. And have you ever tried to ride a hundred miles behind a team of gassy oxen? You'll beg for oxen-gen.

Buffalo Trace was the first road built in the Indiana territory, following a trail already laid by bison from the Ohio River to Vincennes. I'd imagine it didn't smell all that great, either, and I wouldn't want to fight a buffalo for the right of way.

When Corydon became the capital, road construction exploded, and by that I mean a few dusty paths spread out to places like Mauckport—a port, apparently—and New Albany. There was no road to old Albany. Just three years after Indy became Indy, wagons and stagecoaches ran between the new and old state capitals.

It made for a rough ride, to say the least. Still, they were usable year round, except in winter and when there was any amount of moisture on the ground, and never if you had dust allergies. Okay, the roads sucked.

The Feds came to the rescue with the gravel-covered National Road, which I mentioned earlier, but it's hardly the first time I've repeated myself. The National Road came into the state in 1829 and connected the East Coast (Maryland) with the Midwest. In the 30s the Michigan Road came through from, yes, Michigan. Like the National Road it went through Indianapolis, on its way to Kentucky. The two roads became a foundation for a statewide road system. Thus Indy (It's *so* stressful typing out Indianapolis) had a good start on its eventual Crossroads nickname.

It does make one wonder why they bothered with the canals. Can you say "devalued bonds"? Nice try. But a lot more goods could be loaded on a flatboat than a wagon. Abraham Lincoln once got a job as a flatboat crewman, although it's worth a mention that wannabe cargo thieves ambushed his boat during a trip to New Orleans. Surely he took care of them with his ax.

At the time, a canal system seemed a reasonable risk, like a spin-off of "M*A*S*H": Worth a try, and only a disaster in retrospect. But soon, with the canal system underwater and the road system on the wrong path, some way had to be found for reliable mass transportation. Something like … an iron horse.

The buffalo could have used this

In early Indiana, buffalo traces and Indian trails ended at rivers that had to be forded, and with the Wabash, that was a daunting proposition. After the Civil War a bridge was built near the scene of George Rogers Clark's victory over the British at Vincennes. In 1931 it was replaced with this bridge, which takes travelers from Illinois into Indiana—or the other way around, but who would want to do that?

Although Indiana got its first railroad in the late 1830s, it wasn't exactly a transportation revolution. Built in the town of Shelbyville, the train was pulled by a horse and ran about a mile. It was, for all intents, an amusement park ride. Maybe not as exciting as the rides at Indiana Beach, but still.

Only in 1847 was a major line built, connecting Indianapolis with the Ohio River town of Madison. It was called the Madison and Indianapolis. As transportation grew, Indianapolis would too (Madison didn't, as much as Indy, but the firefighter in me needs to point out Madison is protected by the oldest fire company in the state.) Indianapolis started at a population of 8,000 in 1850, and in the next fifty years added another 169,000 people. Bet it was more than a square mile by then.

Pardon me boy, is this the Madison Choo-Choo?

Indiana's first railroad started out from Madison in 1836—after all, it would be silly for the Madison and Indianapolis to start out from Evansville. So it's no surprise to find the Victorian-era Madison Railroad Station, built in 1895 during what I would presume to be the Victorian era. With its octagonal waiting room, it was used as a community center, freight terminal, and then sold to an electrical supply company, but now belongs to the Jefferson County Historical Society. The former tracks are now a roadway, but the building itself is a major historical site within the city's historical district.

The new railroad showed the shape of things to come, and the shape had two long iron rails. Now large amounts of products and people could be shipped long distances at a lower cost, a boon for everyone except hermits who shot deer for food and clothing ... and even they needed to buy lead and gunpowder, from time to time.

So the railroad boomed in the 1850s, and I don't mean literally, although there was a crash or three. Rails went east and west, water went north and south, and everything seemed to meet in the capital, which soon became known as the cross ... well, you know.

Still, by the end of the decade there was no railroad bridge across the Ohio or Mississippi rivers. Remember that, when the time comes for us to talk about the Civil War.

They Were Always A' Workin' On the Railroad

There are a couple of special mentions when it comes to railroads in Indiana and they go here, after the transportation chapter, because ... well ... the transportation chapter got too long.

In 1888 the city of Lafayette, which was named after a guy named Lafayette, became the first in the state to have a completely electrified street railway system. This is something that wouldn't have happened in 1816, for the pretty obvious reason that they didn't have electricity.

That brings me to South Bend, which actually tried it in 1882. They did have electricity—about enough to move a street car a few blocks. A few years later they could take one a couple of miles, but mules were cheaper than electricity, and only shocking if you got too close when they did their business.

But, while electricity had the disadvantage of being electric, the steam engines of main railroad lines were noisy, smoky, and I assume steamy. Just five years after Lafayette got a charge out of railroads, there were 173 miles of electric cars compared to 92 miles of animal drawn cars. The horses and mules voted "neigh", of course.

(My editor informs me that mules don't neigh. When I told her not to get her nickers in a bunch, she said mules don't nicker, either. I'm beginning to question my sense of humor. Guess I'm just whinnying.)

In the city of Anderson a guy named Charles L. Henry—who owned the mule-powered streetcars—named the new electric railways "interurban". He managed to get one going between towns instead of within, with a train that carried passengers between Anderson and Alexandria. New lines soon sprung up to cover the rest of the alphabet.

The interurbans grew to 2,300 miles of tracks, crossing more than 60 of Indiana's 92 counties, but eventually they fell to the same invention that took out so much mass transportation in the country: the automobile. Last time I checked the South Shore, going to and from South Bend and Chicago, was the last one.

An interurban was often more of a local line, like a bus service between neighboring cities compared to an interstate Greyhound. But another railroad line became synonymous with the entire state: the Monon Line.

No? Okay, it's been a few years:

To get why this became so popular, you have to understand just how huge sports became in Indiana—and by that I mean college sports most of all. The Monon line provided passenger service for students going to and from not only the big colleges, like Purdue and Indiana University, but also the many small ones across the state.

The line painted its cars in school colors, and you can imagine how popular it was to take a train between schools on weekends when rival teams were having at each other. Sadly, the Monon line was bought up by around 1970 and closed its passenger service.

I don't have to tell you Indiana became quite the car country later on. I do? Okay then, moving on.

Get along, little dogie

That's the title of a famous cowboy ballad covered by, among others, Roy Rogers, Tex Ritter, and of course Alvin and the Chipmunks. What's a dogie? A motherless calf. Yes, I found that out only while writing this caption.

These cow-people aren't likely to see a little dogie, but there's plenty of other scenery along the saddle trail at Pokagon State Park, near Angola.

Indiana Facts:

INDY AND THE HARRISONS

Three Presidents have a direct connection to Indiana. Two died in office, but otherwise their connections with the Hoosier state are very different.

William Henry Harrison, despite how much we talked about him earlier, was just one of those Presidents. He became our first territorial congressional delegate and governor of the Indiana Territory, kicked Native American butt in the Battle of Tippecanoe, won the War of 1812 Battle of the Thames, then abandoned us for Ohio and became an astronaut.

(Seriously, you have to wonder: Why did so many Buckeyes hate their state so much they willingly climbed on board a tower of rocket fuel to get blasted away from it?)

Harrison was the last President born a British subject, and his father signed the Declaration of Independence before becoming governor of Virginia. Those are pretty big shoes to fill.

He was soaked in history the way I soak myself in bug spray. He roomed with Robert Morris while studying medicine under Benjamin Rush—both signed the Declaration of Independence. He was talked into joining the army by Virginia Governor Henry Lee, a Revolutionary War hero whose son grew up to be Confederate General Robert E. Lee.

Then Harrison went to the Northwest Territory, where he joined the army under the command of Mad Anthony Wayne. This was a man steeped in greatness and destined for greatness, as long as he didn't, you know, die.

On a related note, after being elected President W.H. Harrison delivered the longest inaugural address in American history, even after Daniel Webster edited it. (Yeah, *the* Daniel Webster.) In the cold rain ... with no coat or hat. (Harrison, not Webster.)

Then President Harrison caught a cold and died, a month after getting the job. What nerve. They say weather and illness aren't connected, but when I get elected President, it'll be a very short speech in an overcoat. I'll be in an overcoat, not the speech.

But Harrison had more than one connection to Indiana. In addition to being governor of the territory and a congressional delegate, not to mention doing army stuff all over the area, he also had a son.

That son also had a son. And *that* son, the grandson of the ninth President, became the 23rd President. Oops ... spoiler alert.

So this new Harrison's great-grandfather fought for our independence, and his grandfather fought in what's often called the Second Revolution (The War of 1812), and his father (who was born in Vincennes) served in the U.S. House of Representatives. (He's also the only person so far to be both child and parent of a President, so there's that.) Benjamin Harrison continued that chain of service, and became a colonel of the 70th Indiana during the Civil War.

Harrison (Benjamin, that is) accompanied Sherman in his famous March to the Sea, but it might be best not to mention that to your southern friends. He also made it to the rank of General before the war ended, then went back to Indiana and got himself elected Reporter of the Indiana Supreme Court.

Sure, there are more exciting positions, but it was a start ... and a paycheck.

Harrison worked his way up to be the nominee for governor in 1872, which he promptly lost. But four years later the Republican nominee for President dropped out at the last minute, and Harrison stepped up with the campaign promise of, "I'll serve longer than grandpa did!"

He lost.

Eventually he did become a Senator, then ran for reelection. And lost.

But the Harrisons are nothing if not stubborn, and on the eighth ballot in 1888 he received the Republican nomination for President, again. He won the north and the west, while President Grover Cleveland took the south. Voter turnout: 79.3%! Cleveland won the popular vote by a margin of 90,000, but Harrison took the Electoral College and the election.

So there you go, Indiana's President Benjamin Harrison, the last President with a full beard and the second to shortest (after Madison). Shortest body, not beard. His beard grew longer than he was tall, so to avoid the fate of his grandfather he wrapped it around his body during wet weather. It's possible I'm exaggerating, but it's true his inauguration speech was half as long as William Henry Harrison's. Better safe.

Harrison had a busy presidency, and among other things he tried to get legislation passed to protect the civil rights of black Americans. He also took time out to be the first President to have his voice preserved, on a wax phonograph cylinder. He had the White House wired for electricity for the first time—but Harrison, a brave Civil War veteran, was so afraid of the newfangled electricity that he and his wife would sleep with the lights on, afraid to touch the switches.

He also expanded the navy and started the process of annexing Hawaii, which didn't go over well with all the Hawaiians but—yay, Hawaii!

Eventually Harrison died, which tends to happen to people, and was buried in Crown Hill Cemetery in Indianapolis. Both his wives were buried next to him (they weren't married at the same time). That could make for some uncomfortable spirit gatherings.

So, overall, he didn't do too badly. He got his statue, and a ship named after him, and there's Fort Benjamin Harrison in Lawrence, Indiana. Well, there was, but now it's a state park.

Oh, and the third President I mentioned earlier? He just kind of passed through Indiana on his way to Illinois. Why is he more remembered? Well, he had the more interesting name: Abraham Lincoln. He might deserve his own section.

A hundred years to a billion

Benjamin Harrison was called the centennial president: He was inaugurated in 1893, a century after the first inauguration of George Washington. On a darker note, he was president when federal spending reached a billion dollars for the first time, an issue that led to his reelection defeat.

Harrison was happier at his home in Indianapolis, constructed in 1874 on North Delaware Street. It later served as a rooming house, then female dormitory for the Jordan Conservatory of Music.

Chapter Eight:
A MORNING CONSTITUTIONAL

Let's go back a bit: Who said history had to be linear?

Oh. That many people, huh?

We'll only go back to 1831, then. That's when the state decided to build the first state capitol building designed to be an actual state capitol building. They'd moved the capital to Indianapolis in 1825, but set up shop in the Marion County Courthouse. A nice enough place, but a little busy, what with county court and government work going on, and all.

The new capitol design was inspired by the Greek Parthenon. This may seem un-American but, after all, we don't have a Parthenon of our own. As this is written the Greeks are deep within a financial crisis—it's too bad that couldn't have been predicted—and although the Parthenon is paid for, there are certain parallels.

The state (of Indiana, not Greece) had already suffered through a financial crisis in 1819, only three years into statehood. Imagine what they would have done with credit cards. Early governors William Hendricks and Noah Noble had their hands full, just trying to fix Indiana's finances. The state's credit rating was so bad that if the local Native Americans could have come up with the cash they'd have bought us out, and today we'd have a casino for *them* to gamble at.

But finally everything was back in black, and our financial future looked to be okay as long as we didn't start hiring Greek architects. Hard work made us solvent.

So naturally the state started overspending again, on the mammoth projects mentioned earlier.

The resulting deficit was funded by state bonds—in no way is this a comment on current events—and by the sale of nine million acres of public land. Shockingly, the overspending and debt couldn't be sustained, and soon Indiana owned the same amount of money as it took in over the entire first fifteen years of statehood.

In the end, the state signed over public works in exchange for a 50% reduction in debt, but only the population boom and private enterprise eventually got Indiana back on financial track.

Okay, maybe this is a comment on current events, just a little.

The new building lasted until 1878, when it was torn down and replaced by a two million dollar structure that still stands today, at least last time I checked.

Lots of other changes came along. For instance, during the 1840s the state named after Indians finished kicking out the Indians. Some went voluntarily, but we can also brag of something called the Potawatomi Trail of Death, which was just as fun and frivolous as the name suggests. There's still a Pokagon Band of the Potawatomi—some of this book was written at Pokagon State Park—but most of the natives moved on, as far north as Canada and as far west as Kansas.

You'd think they would have repaired the crack

In 1950, the federal government gave each state a replica of the famous Liberty Bell, as a way of encouraging the sale of savings bonds. I wonder how many bonds it took to purchase 48 bells? And did Alaska and Hawaii each get one later?

The state changed so much it soon became clear the original State Constitution didn't cut it anymore. Critics didn't like the fact that so many state positions were appointed instead of elected, and new political parties could take advantage of the way it was written. It had never been voted on by the general public, as there basically was no general public in 1816.

So, in 1851, a constitutional convention was called, because what else would you call it? It took only a year for the delegates to slap the thing together, but it must have worked, because the public voted it in. It's been Indiana's State Constitution ever since.

Not that there haven't been changes in it. In fact, the delegates might have saved themselves some trouble by waiting another fifteen years, as the new Constitution didn't deal with free blacks ... on the contrary, it put more restrictions on them. In Indiana, a free state, black people couldn't testify in court against whites, and black children went to separate schools.

We can take some small comfort in the fact that, at around the same time, Indiana began to play a vital role in guiding former slaves to freedom through the Underground Railroad. That might help explain why at one time

Indianapolis had a higher black population than any other northern city, and why it's considered the least segregated city in the north to this day.

On the other hand, we can take no comfort at all in the later rise of the Ku Klux Klan, a pasty-faced group that would become huge in Indiana.

A huge joke. Okay, not that funny.

Indiana Facts:

"HE'S OUR PRESIDENT! NO, HE'S OURS!"

Three states can lay claim to Abraham Lincoln. You could say he was born in Kentucky, grew up in Indiana, and did all his adult stuff as an Illinois resident.

Well, you can say it if you want—who am I to stop you? It's a free country, partially thanks to Abe.

A lot of the stuff you hear about Abe Lincoln is, surprisingly, true. His family got to America in 1637, and Thomas Lincoln's father, the original Abraham, moved his family to Kentucky in 1782. So it took them almost 150 years to reach the Bluegrass State and produce little Abe, but hey—travel took longer back then.

Unfortunately, four years after they arrived Grandpa Abe Lincoln was killed by American Indians, because, after all, he stepped on their proverbial lawn. But Thomas grew up, married Nancy Hanks, and bought a farm near Hodgenville. Hodgenville is south of Louisville along the Lincoln Parkway, although it's safe to assume the highway didn't exist at the time.

The foundation of Abe Lincoln's boyhood

It's all well and good to visit the farm rebuilt to look exactly like Abraham Lincoln's boyhood home. But not far away you can see the actual, honest to goodness real place. The remains of it, anyway.

Here stood the original cabin. You can almost see little Abe over by the fireplace, using a charred stick to draw his math on the back of a shovel, and cursing the next morning when he realizes he has to shovel out the barn with his homework.

Just like in the stories, Abraham Lincoln was born in a one-room log cabin, and later attended school in a log schoolhouse. They laid a lot of logs back then.

In 1816—the same year Indiana became a state—the Lincoln family crossed the Ohio River and settled in Indiana. Abe was six, so we Hoosiers can claim some of his formative years.

And formative they were. At age seven he shot a wild turkey, which upset him so much he never hunted again. It was February, after all, and with no way to keep the turkey until next Thanksgiving, it was wasted.

The next year he got kicked in the head by a horse, and for a time everyone thought he was dead. Personally, that would have put me back on to shooting animals. That same year his mother did die, permanently, from a medical condition called milk sickness.

Nancy Lincoln's Gravestone
Although born in Kentucky and buried in Illinois, Abraham Lincoln left the best part of himself in Indiana: his mother. Nancy Hanks Lincoln was buried here after dying of milk sickness, from cows who eat the white snakeroot plant. Her last known words about her now-famous son were: "He never writes, he never brings a flatboat down to visit ..."
There is no validity to the rumor that Abe Lincoln's last words to Nancy were: "Calm down, Ma, I'll visit soon. Here, have some milk."

Like Lincoln, milk sickness was uniquely American—this is the only continent it happened on. It came when cows ate a plant called white snakeroot, and wouldn't you think the name alone would keep the cows away from it? That's why learning to read is so important. Today milk sickness is almost unheard of, so we use fast cars to control the population.

Lincoln didn't attend school much, but he developed a love for reading and would borrow books whenever he could. This was because they had no electricity for his PlayStation. You can't power a videogame console with candles, but you can sure as heck read by them.

He also got to travel a bit, something many people never did. In 1828 he helped crew a flatboat down the Mississippi, and got his first taste of slavery when he saw a slave auction in progress. During the same trip seven black men tried to rob the flatboat, which could be called ironic. After he fought them off Lincoln didn't hold a grudge.

Then, in 1830, the Lincoln family moved 200 miles, into Illinois. Abraham Lincoln was never heard from again.

Okay, not really. In fact, that same year Lincoln made his first speech, which urged navigation improvements on the Sangamon River, near Decatur. Over the next several years he read, enlisted in the military, read, ran a business into the ground, read, became a postmaster, got elected to the state legislature, and realized he'd read so much he could start studying law.

So it all worked out pretty well for him.

Okay, there were

Is it just me, or is it leaning a little?
An exacting reproduction of Abe Lincoln's boyhood home shows the family didn't have a whole lot of extra space for, say, an indoor swimming pool, except possibly during heavy rains. I was a little awed just to walk on the property. I'm easily awed, though.

bumps along the way. He had bouts of depression, lost an election, was unlucky in love, and almost got into a sword duel. All because he left Indiana, so let that be a lesson to you.

Abe went to the well just often enough
While most of the Lincoln Boyhood National Memorial is an authentic reproduction of life for the future president, a little extra walk will bring you to the real thing. Abe Lincoln came to this very well, and drew actual water, and actually drank, and stuff. I'd be lying if I didn't admit to being just a little awed by that. I didn't cry, though. Don't ask my wife.

In 1900 Lincoln's son, Todd, gave $1,000 to take care of his grandmother's Indiana grave. Spencer County officials gave another $800, and bought 16 acres around the gravesite. That place is now the Lincoln Boyhood National Memorial. I understand there's also a monument for him in Washington.

Chapter Nine:
YOU CALL THIS CIVIL?

By the time the Civil War reared its extremely ugly head, the population of Indiana had reached a million. Good thing too, because the state played a critical role in the conflict.

Entire books, and series of books, have been written about the American Civil War, also known to some as the War of Northern Aggression. (You can guess where those some live.) Since this is a humor book, and there's not much funny about a war, we'll just cover the basics of Indiana's role.

(Yes, it is a humor book. It *is*. You haven't figured that out after eight chapters?)

Regiments from Indiana participated in every major battle, and almost all the battles, major or minor, that took place in the west. In fact, Hoosiers provided 126 infantry regiments, 26 artillery batteries, and 13 cavalry regiments. In the initial call for troops, so many Hoosiers volunteered that many got turned away. By the end, over 208,000 men (and an unknown number of cross-dressing women) served from Indiana, and took 35% casualties.

Before it was done, 15% of the state's population served in the military—approaching the voter turnout in today's off-year elections.

Come to Indiana, We'll Get You Killed

Before the war, much of Indiana's population lived in the southern half of the state, and much of that came from even further south. My own family arrived from the Carolinas, by way of Tennessee and Kentucky. When my relatives drive a car that starts sliding on ice, they don't know whether to yell, "Well, typical winter" or "Hey y'all, watch this".

That being the case, a lot of southern sympathizers lived in the state. They were called Copperheads, because they were thought of as snakes in the grass. What did the grass ever do to them, anyway? Indiana Democrats, spinning their views as antiwar rather than proslavery, insisted the term actually stood for the copper Liberty head on a penny. They would cut the heads from copper pennies and wear them as badges, thus defacing federal currency. They quickly dropped that practice years later, when Lincoln's head ended up on the penny and suddenly it didn't seem so very pro-South.

The Copperhead movement collapsed in September of 1864, when Union troops in Atlanta captured the South's main copper storage facility and replaced the Liberty head on pennies with a smiley face.

On the other side of the Ohio River, Governor Beriah Mogoffin of Kentucky did his best to keep the state neutral. (That's his real name, by the way—I didn't sneeze while typing it.) He refused to allow Union troops to mobilize in his state, which sounds pretty bad until you realize he wouldn't let Confederate troops mobilize there, either.

Indiana Governor Morton, in his salt of the earth way (get it? Morton? Salt? Never mind.), poured himself into the gap. He simply invited Kentuckians to come up to Indiana and enlist. Many of them did just that, joining Hoosier units at places such as Camp Joe Holt in Jeffersonville (right across the river from Louisville). Joe Holt was Secretary of War in the Buchanan administration—for two months. Later Lincoln made Holt Judge Advocate General of the Union Army, and he was prosecutor during the Lincoln assassination trials.

By the way, if you ever want to visit Fort Joe Holt, it's now the interpretive center at the Falls of the Ohio State Park.

As time went by a Confederate state government came to Kentucky, but no one told the Union state government, which didn't go anywhere. The Confederates admitted Kentucky to their union, but the North never let it go, and most of the state's residents weren't interested in joining the land of cotton. To this day the population of Frankfort (North) and Bowling Green (South) argue over who had the better state seal, song, and ... don't get me started on the flag.

Although the Confederates did capture Frankfort, their inauguration ceremony of the new government got interrupted by party crashers—an army under Union General Don Carlos Buell. Afterward the Confederate capital of Kentucky moved to ... Tennessee.

Through his efforts to keep his southern neighbor in the Union and to recruit troops from there, Morton was sometimes called "Governor of Indiana *and* Kentucky". That may have irritated Beriah Magoffin. But Magoffin, a Southern sympathizer with a pro-Union legislature, had problems of his own ... even if you didn't count his name.

At least 2,000 Kentuckians came to Camp Joe Holt, where they formed the Fifth Kentucky Volunteer Infantry Regiment. Turns out Morton was pretty smart: Forming recruitment camps inside Kentucky might have just irritated the situation more.

It isn't certain how many Hoosiers might have gone south to join the Confederate army, but plenty of people in the state had Southern roots. In fact, Indiana Senator Jesse D. Bright got himself kicked out of the US Senate when he wrote to Confederate President Jefferson Davis, and offered to sell the South guns in return for a vacation package in Boca Raton, Florida.

Opening a Can of Raid

Indiana regiments fought just about everywhere during the war, except for Indiana—usually. The 14th Indiana infantry regiment took Cemetery Hill on the first day of the Battle of Gettysburg. An all-black infantry regiment, the 28th Indiana, lost 212 men in less than a year. The 19th Indiana Infantry, part of the Iron Brigade, fought in the second Battle of Bull Run and on through the war, until they were almost wiped out at Gettysburg.

This might be a good time to point out the third largest military hospital in the North was in Jeffersonville, not far from Fort Joe Holt.

But usually Hoosier units headed elsewhere. On July 18, 1862, a Confederate Colonel named Adam Ranking "Stovepipe" Johnson decided to change that.

Stovepipe Johnson. Wow.

Johnson led his troops to Newburgh, Indiana (just south of Oldburgh), a large river port along the Ohio. There was a Union garrison there, but Johnson got them to surrender by threatening to shell the town with his cannon.

That's no stovepipe!
A Union cannon stands by at the Ligonier Stone's Trace Pioneer Festival, ready to open a case of whoop—hey, wait. Judging from the flag behind it, maybe Johnny Reb sneaked a little further north than we thought.

You can imagine the Union embarrassment when it turned out Johnson didn't have any cannons. Instead he found some stovepipes, and camouflaged them to look like something a lot more dangerous. Looks like I just found the origin of his nickname.

Realizing he was from the South and didn't need stovepipes, Johnson soon withdrew. But the raids weren't over: Hines would soon catchup.

Thomas Hines led a Confederate force into Indiana in June, 1863, with orders to lay the groundwork for a bigger raid later. Part of Hines' job was to see what support they would get from Hoosier Copperheads. He gathered his men in Woodbury, Tennessee, and told them they were in for a long, dangerous mission. He explained that he couldn't say where they would go, but that before they volunteered they should know neither the North nor the South had yet approved riverboat gambling.

The men volunteered anyway. They stole Union uniforms, robbed a train for Union cash, and gambled on stealing a riverboat to cross the Ohio River near Derby, Indiana. They headed to Paoli, where townspeople, grateful for the protection of Union troops, fed them a big meal.

Unfortunately, during that meal the real Union troops showed up.

The counterfeit Confederates managed to get away and headed to French Lick, where they almost got caught again when they paused too long to giggle over the town's name. There they did some wheeling and dealing with a local Copperhead, who expected to raise a local force of 10,000 Copperhead volunteers, but Hines had to flee again before the deal could be closed.

The good looking bad guys went to Valeene, where everyone still thought they were Union troops. But then the occupants of a home refused to give them dinner, so they set the house on fire.

This proved a bone-headed move. "Gee," the residents said, "why would Union troops set fire to a northerner's house? Were they really that hungry?"

The game was up, so Hines hired a local man named Bryant Breeden to guide his troops to safety.

Unfortunately, Hines didn't first bother to make sure Breeden was a Copperhead. He wasn't. Breeden guided the men to Little Blue Island, in the middle of the Ohio River. You have to think—wouldn't the gray troops be a little suspicious of being led to a blue island?

In the end Hines got away, but most of his force was captured and, without ever setting foot on a floating casino, they lost the bet. Eventually Hines reported back to Morgan that they could expect little help from Indiana, and as a result John Hunt Morgan didn't treat Hoosiers very nicely when he embarked on *his* raid.

You'd think, after two raids and nothing to show for it but stovepipes, they'd have given up.

Just Don't Make Fun of French Lick, and You'll Be Okay

John Hunt Morgan led 2,400 cavalry troopers toward Indiana on July 8, 1863. They found, waiting along the Ohio River shore, a group of the local guard, part of the 6th Regiment of the Indiana Legion. The Indiana Legion was basically a (slightly) organized militia unit, only with a cooler name.

Legion members stood on the north bank of the Ohio, thumbed their noses, and shouted, "You shall not pass!" But Morgan didn't have only horses: His stovepipes were real cannons. He fired across the river, and by the time he got to the north side found nothing but mud and some good fishing worms.

The militia, meanwhile, fell back toward nearby Corydon, where a larger group—you could say a legion—was on the way. Corydon, you'll recall, served as the original capital of Indiana, so there was a certain historical pride in protecting it.

The Indiana Legion had no idea how many Confederates were Confederating and faced them near the river, outnumbered more than 20-1. Soon the rest of the 6th Regiment arrived to start building a defensive line. Now they were outnumbered by only around 5-1.

The Confederates tried a frontal attack, then a flanking attack, with little success. The Union soldiers thumbed their noses and said, "We're king of the breastworks, you can't get us". They were unaware only the forward units had attacked so far.

When the rest of the Southern troops arrived with their artillery (real, not stovepipe), the Legion had to fall back. Even then many got captured as they tried to get out of town. Although the Confederates lost twice as many men as the North, they could still claim a victory. They stuck around long enough to loot the area of supplies and money, because no one could possibly be on the way to take them on, right?

Just the same, Morgan wasn't in a celebratory mood. While eating lunch in Corydon, he learned that days earlier the Confederate armies suffered severe losses at Gettysburg and Vicksburg. Luckily, he hadn't landed in a town that ended in "burg".

He did take time to do one smart thing: Morgan spread false messages to show he was headed north to Indianapolis, to raid Camp Morton and free Confederate prisoners there. He'd considered doing that, but changed his mind when he realized the South wasn't exactly on a roll at the moment.

While Morgan continued his raid, Governor Morton contacted the War Department with the following message. "Bad guys here. Send our Indiana Regiments back. Please?"

General Burnside, he who made sideburns popular, sent a cavalry unit to help. But Morton shouldn't have worried, because when he called out all available militia units, word got around. In the next week, more than 150,000 Hoosiers showed up, saying, "I love the name: *Indiana Legion.* Now, give me a gun and point me toward those Johnny Rebs who looted our old capital."

Instead of heading toward Indianapolis—which would have been a truly boneheaded move—Morgan raided the town of Salem and then turned east. He'd stuck his hand into a beehive, and in addition to the militia, 6,000 Union cavalry troops were now on his tail. Just as Morgan caused the only pitched Civil War battle in Indiana, he also plunged into the biggest battle of the war in Ohio, where he got caught on Buffington Island while trying to escape back across the Ohio River. Over half his men were captured there, while Morgan headed north with the rest.

A lady always travels with an escort

Although the South managed a few incursions into Indiana during the Civil War, they'd be jealous to know these Confederate soldiers (and their accompanying Southern belle) made it all the way to the northeastern part of the state. Luckily, it wasn't an invasion: these reenactors attended the 2015 Stone's Trace Festival, near Ligonier.

Chased by troops from much of the former Northwest Territory (Michigan, Illinois, Indiana, and Ohio, in addition to Kentucky and even Tennessee), he engaged in the northernmost battle involving an organized Confederate unit of the Civil War, at Salineville, Ohio.

(A pitched battle is kind of an organized conflict between two armed groups, as opposed to a siege or a skirmish. In this case, pitch has nothing at all to do with baseball. Northern General Abner Doubleday, who gets possibly

75

false credit for inventing baseball, was not present, and Morgan came nowhere close to hitting a home run.)

Morgan finally surrendered to an Ohio Militia captain named Burbridge, a man he'd earlier captured. They must have struck a deal, because Burbridge immediately pardoned Morgan and his officers—an action that would have allowed Morgan's troops to return home to Kentucky, technically as civilians.

Unfortunately for Morgan, it turned out Burbridge was really James Burbick, and Burbick was not an officer in anything. As a result, Morgan became very familiar with the Ohio Penitentiary.

The Corydon Battle Site is now on the National Register of Historic Places, part of the John Hunt Morgan Heritage Trail. Every year the battle of Corydon is reenacted by men portraying the Indiana militia, who stand at the town limits and repeat the famous last words of a free John Hunt Morgan:

"Well, maybe we'll do better in Pennsylvania."

Indiana Facts:

THE BATTLE OF POGUE'S RUN, OR: YOU THINK POLITICS ARE BAD *NOW*

It may come as some surprise that at the time of the Civil War the Democrat majority in the state legislature, including its head, were southern sympathizers. They didn't want to help the war effort—at least, not the northern war effort.

So Governor Oliver Morton and the minority Republicans did it themselves. They kept the legislature from assembling for two years and borrowed money, even though they couldn't. In other words, they broke the law.

Lanier on the Ohio

Franklin Doughty Lanier loaned over a million dollars to Indiana Governor Morton, which allowed Morton to outfit Indiana troops during the Civil War. Shouldn't a man like that have a house named after him? Sure enough, architect Francis Costigan designed the Lanier mansion, which overlooks recreated 19th century gardens and the Ohio River, in Madison. It's now a National Historical Landmark and open to the public, but that's okay—Lanier doesn't live there anymore.

In the end, this resulted in a battle right there in Indianapolis: The Battle of Pogue's Run.

On May 20, 1863, Indiana Democrats assembled in Indianapolis for their state convention. Governor Morton got word his opponents planned to overthrow the Indiana government—I mean, why not fight illegality with illegality? So Morton rounded up some Union troops and headed them toward the convention. What could possibly go wrong?

About 10,000 Democrats were at the convention when less than a dozen soldiers entered, rifles cocked and bayonets fixed. (I didn't know they were broken.) That got everyone's attention.

The convention goers decided discretion was the batter part of a gun battle, so they split the scene. In their eagerness to have a ball, but not a Minie ball (It's a Civil War era bullet ... never mind), the escaping crowd pushed down a fence along the statehouse square, only to encounter a cavalry squad galloping in their direction.

The tumult attracted the attention of a Union Colonel named Coburn, who was on security duty nearby. He talked the soldiers down, and the convention broke up after declaring the Governor had two wars on his hands: One against the South, and one against the Constitution.

Some soldiers continued to be a problem, and used scare tactics on anyone who spoke against the war. Later that night, as the Democrats headed home, some of them fired shots from train cars heading toward Lafayette and Terra Haute. Union soldiers responded by positioning a cannon in front of a suspect train, which as you might imagine convinced the crew to stop.

In quick succession, guns showed up in droves: About forty taken from those arrested at the convention; about two hundred found on the train; and somewhere between 500-2,000 thrown from another train into Pogue's Run. Seven pistols were hidden in the petticoats of one woman, in the theory no one would search her; the soldiers got suspicious when she kept clinking.

Turns out the Democrats *were* armed, to the teeth. You have to wonder what would have happened if they'd turned all those guns on that first group of soldiers, then outnumbered by something like 1,000 to one.

The term "spin" may not have existed then, but it still happened. Republicans praised the soldiers, saying they broke up a meeting of traitors. The Democrats spun it as another assault on Constitutional Rights; It could be argued they were both right. The good thing is this particular battle resulted in no casualties.

Afterward Republican Jonathan Jennings got elected Governor and declared Indiana a free state, which ended talk of secession—but didn't end cross-party feuding. After his terms in the Governor's mansion Jennings slummed it for a time, serving 18 years in the US Congress.

Site of the Battle of Pogue's Run, only 25 years later

Hoosiers are traditional people, traditionally, yet this is the fifth building to house the state government. The first, in Corydon, still stands, but the second and third were torn down so we could get it right. (The fourth was the Supreme Court office building, which got crowded real fast while the fifth was being built.)

$2 million was budgeted for the new building, but Governor Williams was a notorious miser, and when it was completed in 1888 he returned $100,000 to the budget. The doors were made of Indiana oak, with limestone from you-know-where used throughout. The new statehouse was also wired for electricity— even though at the time Indianapolis didn't have an electrical power grid. When completed, it was the second highest building in the state.

Chapter Ten:
IT'S THE ECONOMY, STUPID

Although cities further north saw economic growth from supply and military activity, the Midwest's highway—the Ohio River—remained closed by the war for four years.

I mean, the water kept flowing—let's not get silly. But shipping was limited because ships on the river tended to have cannon balls shot at them. River cities suffered an economic decline, and the cheap gas that saw central Indiana boom later on never really floated down to them. (I'll get plenty of mileage later from the cheap gas jokes.)

Attracted to the transportation possibilities of the Great Lakes and the railroads, much of the population moved north, and after the war they tended to stay there. This added new words to the Hoosier lexicon, such as "snow belt", "lake effect", and "&$*#@*%& winter!"

Before the Civil War, Indiana's largest city was New Albany, along the Ohio. (It's near Clarksville, the place you can take the last train to.) In addition to their economy suffering from the loss of trade, they were a bit too friendly with the South, and when it was all over the area fell out of favor. Were they really Southern sympathizers? Well, they had a booming steamboat building business in town, and the last steamboat built there, in 1870, was named the *Robert E. Lee*. So... maybe.

But while New Albany stagnated, the war brought an explosion in Indiana industry (and I don't mean that literally. Not usually). Factories and businesses rose along the Great Lakes; since a sliver of Lake Michigan touches Hoosier shores, Indiana got its share of access. The meeting of railroads in central Indiana was another factor.

Meanwhile, veterans returned from the Civil War and started businesses or otherwise made their mark. Indianapolis already had Dr. Richard Gatling, who invented one of the world's first machine guns as a way to increase his customer base.

Colonel Eli Lilly came to the city and founded a company he called, not shockingly, Eli Lilly and Company, which became the state's largest corporation. He was a drug dealer. I mean, in a good way, as in he manufactured medications.

Charles Conn left the war and the south and headed all the way up to Elkhart, where he started an industry building musical instruments. He didn't want to get too close to Dr. Gatling, whose product was not music to his ears. Elkhart became known throughout the world as a center of non-gunfire music.

Major General Lew Wallace fought in both the Mexican-American War and the Civil War and had a political career, but the Covington native is better known for his six novels, including *Ben-Hur*. I don't know if the book was better, but Charlton Heston chewed scenery in the movie version.

Ambrose Burnside was already mentioned briefly, as the Union General who refused to send Indiana infantry regiments to aid the state during Morgan's Raid. But Burnside himself was a Hoosier, born in Liberty—both literally and figuratively. Finding the state too big, he later became governor of Rhode Island.

Of course, you already know about Brigadier General Benjamin Harrison.

Baby, it's coal outside

An observation tower at Clifty Falls State Park yields a look at two big factors in the southern Indiana economy: coal and the Ohio River. Beyond that: the hills of Kentucky.

Another Hoosier Civil War veteran was Jefferson Davis. No, not *that* Jefferson Davis: Colonel Jefferson Columbus Davis, who did indeed head south, but for a whole different reason than his Confederate counterpart. This Davis took part in Sherman's March to the Sea.

Sorry, we were talking about the economy. Before the Civil War, to be frank, we were all farmers. But the shortage of manpower during the war resulted in mechanization, and that caused big changes.

The number of farms doubled in the three decades after the war, but other businesses boomed even more. Indiana had natural resources, good transportation, and to quote Mohammed Ali, we were pretty. Toward the end of the 1890s Indiana produced more steel than any state—a quarter of the entire national output. Of course, these days everyone wants to make their steel out of plastic.

Harvesting dust

A farmer works in his northeast Indiana field, racing against the onset of winter. Indiana ranks 5th nationally in corn production; 4th in soybeans; 2nd in popcorn and tomatoes; 4th in peppermint; 2nd in layer chickens and 3rd in eggs; and 1st in ducks. And, sometimes, 1st in allergens.

The boom also brought the Great Migration to Indiana, as European immigrants joined black and white southerners in a major population shift. This writer (that would be me) later benefited from this, as my family moved from the Appalachian area of Kentucky and Tennessee to northern Indiana. I curse them every winter.

Cheap gas was a large part of the reason U.S. Steel and other companies set up shop in Indiana, and I'm not talking cheap gas jokes. US Steel founded Gary, Indiana as a base for their plant in 1906; decades later the Jackson 5 emerged from that city, so steel manufacturing is directly responsible for Michael Jackson.

In nearby South Bend, the Oliver Farm Equipment Company started up. They brought growth to the town as they manufactured, yes, farm equipment. In fact, they made more plows than any other company in the country.

We'll talk about gas later, hopefully without giggling, but it brought many companies to the state. Among them was the Ball Corporation, which opened in Muncie and became famous for its glass jars. If your mother or grandmother ever canned, chances are they were having a Ball. If your daughter or granddaughter attended Ball State University, they were also on the Ball.

From an economic standpoint, surely Eli Lilly was the most influential of Civil War veterans. The pharmaceutical company he founded went global, with offices in 17 countries and products that ship to 125 countries—although it's still headquartered in Indy. Lilly was the first company to mass produce penicillin, the polio vaccine, and insulin, and last year they made so much money you'd think they could give me just a little.

All this from a man who stayed in the South after the war—for a while. Eli Lilly tried becoming a cotton farmer in Mississippi, but he didn't cotton to the job. He headed north, to a Paris, Illinois drugstore, then came to Indianapolis in 1876 when he got the idea of naming a company after himself.

It worked out for him.

By 1917 Lilly ran the largest capsule factory in the world, producing 2.5 million capsules a day, presumably with medication in them. It became the first drug company to, literally, sugar-coat it. Associated with Nobel Prize winning scientists, the company thrived during the Great Depression and mass-produced necessary drugs, blood plasma, and antiseptics during World War II.

There are many, many successful business ventures in Indiana, of which Lilly is just one big example. If Lilly seems to come up a lot, I should add the company saved my life by developing the antibiotic erythromycin.

Or, at least, they made me way less miserable.

They also introduced Cialis and Prozac so, one way or another, they've made a lot of people very happy, and kept computer spammers very busy.

There were other Hoosier business pioneers. For instance, William Johnson, who invented a process for casting aluminum, and Elwood Haynes, who took his first automobile on the road in 1894 and started the Haynes-Apperson Auto Company two years later.

Later changes in industry would make Indiana part of the Rust Belt, which is just as bad as it sounds, but we don't want to end this part on a down note so I won't mention that.

Wait, I did mention it. Maybe I should bring up the Panic of 1893? No, maybe not. Just the same, by 1925 farmers took a back seat to industry in Indiana employment, even though all those factory workers continued to eat.

There was also the occasional strike, of course. Streetcar workers in Indianapolis went on strike in October, 1913, and demanded Governor Samuel Ralston call in the General Assembly to pass a bill on their behalf. The strike came on the eve of city elections, which the strikers no doubt thought would bring attention to their cause.

They were right. City residents, unable to get to the polls, were outraged, and not at the governor. Ralston did indeed call someone out: the Indiana National Guard. But in the end Ralston promised to negotiate if the strikers went back to work, which they did while insisting it had nothing to do with all those soldiers and guns. The result was Indiana's earliest labor protection laws, and maybe the soldiers got some good practice for the war that would break out a year later, and involve them a few years after that.

Indiana became a leader in automobile and rail car manufacturing, and in making steel and iron which, of course, ended up in automobiles and railroad cars.

Well, This is Depressing

All good things must come to an end, or in this case a pause. Just as the gas and oil slowed to a standstill, so in the 30s did the economy. While FDR struggled with the Great Depression in Washington, Indiana Governor Paul V. McNutt faced Hoosier unemployment rates that reached 25% overall, and more than 50% at times in the southern part of the state.

We have McNutt to thank for Indiana's first income tax, but in other areas he cut taxes in an attempt to stimulate the economy. It didn't work. Railroads went bankrupt, banks failed, and manufacturing basically stopped. Strikes broke out, which forced McNutt to declare martial law, and overall he just didn't have any fun at all.

(This might be a good time to point out McNutt was really the governor's name, honest. It's in the great tradition of odd Indiana names: There's also former Fort Wayne Mayor Harry Baals—he made it very clear that the pronunciation was "Balls"—and the resort town French Lick. French Lick is in tasty Orange County, which also boasts—on the side—the aromatic community of Bacon.)

You'd think the Federal Government would just hand people money and send them home, but things were more reasoned back then: the Federal Works Progress Administration, rather shockingly, put people to work. Not only that, but in jobs that actually did something. Some 75,000 Hoosiers built roads, bridges, and water plants, worked on flood control projects, and did other things that actually made sense.

Granted, it didn't stop the Depression, but it did keep people from starving and gave their lives some meaning. From the Feds! Shocking, in a good way.

What did end the Great Depression, unfortunately, was a Great War.

Oh, I CCC

The Civilian Conservation Corps was a federal work relief program that provided jobs across the country during the Great Depression. In addition to planting three billion trees, CCC workers made improvements in state parks across the country. Here their quality shows at Pokagon State Park in Steuben County, where the CCC Shelter has stood since 1936. Part of this book was written there—appropriate, considering the building is on the National Register of Historic

Indiana Facts:

HOOSIERS HAD GAS

It's hard to drive by the central Indiana community of Gas City without thinking: "Huh? What, is this a big agricultural area—the nation's Bean Basket?"

Um, no. Like Speedway, Gas City gets its name from a specific source, in this case the Trenton Gas Field. You want to put out the cigarette before you go walk near something with a name like that, fella.

You can make gas out of corn, but you can't make corn out of gas

When driving down Interstate 69, I don't stop at Gas City. There lies asphyxiation. But now that we know the gas that fueled the city actually ran out decades ago, why not do the tourist thing? Don't forget to visit their museum.

It all started when natural gas was discovered across a large part of central Indiana. It extended into Ohio, but we don't care about them. Hoosiers, of course, quickly took advantage of the ...

Nah. Hoosiers ignored it for almost a decade, not realizing what bubbled beneath them like a bad chimichanga.

In 1876, coal miners in Eaton dug down to 600 feet, only to find foul gas spewing at them like some hungover dragon with halitosis. They plugged the hole and fled, some convinced they'd torn a hole through the ceiling of Hell. Do you want to stick around when the devil finds a gap in his tile ceiling?

But in 1884 those Ohioans we cavalierly disregarded earlier announced the discovery of natural gas.

It turned out to be the largest natural gas deposit to date, and explorers soon realized it was accompanied by the first big oil reserve in US history. One billion barrels of oil is nothing to sneeze at, unless you're allergic to oil.

Even after they realized what they had, developers continued to waste their chance with it. In their eagerness to get at the oil, companies would vent the natural gas and simply burn it off, bragging that as long as the torch burned, they had oil. Which was true enough in its own way, but didn't take into consideration that the torch might someday stop burning.

Pretty soon wells got drilled in every place but the kitchen sink, and maybe there. Natural gas became so abundant the state government offered it for free, to any industry that agreed to locate to Indiana. No such thing as a free lunch? Don't be silly—eat here and get gas.

Apparently it never occurred to anyone they all drank from the same cup—or maybe siphoned from the same tank.

Remember, Ohio took from it, too. It was also called the Lima-Indiana field, which fits our bean theme but in this case means the city of Lima, in the Buckeye State. So there, Ohio.

(This is the low-brow humor portion of our tale, so go ahead and laugh … I don't judge.)

The free gas (okay, that's enough, stop laughing) attracted numerous companies to the area, especially in the glass and automotive industries. It takes a lot of heat to make glass—something about melting sand. Thus, the Ball Brothers made their mark on the glass industry, and their prosperity gave rise to the city of Muncie, which gave rise to Ball State University, which David Letterman attended, and thus the need for cheap gas jokes.

Big industries attracted supporting companies. That meant construction companies and retail stores, and they all needed workers. There were probably lawyers, too. Good times were being had by all, and it changed Indiana in fundamental ways; after all, even if the gas should happen to run out, the buildings and the people would still be there. Until then, Indiana became an economic paradise as it skipped into the 20th century.

Then someone noticed the big torches turn into little candles. By 1912 it was as if some giant birthday boy finished his wishes; by 1920 nobody had gas, and by 1930 the oil ran out, too.

But the fundamental change was permanent, and as huge as the one caused by the Civil War has been. To this day Indiana is thought of as a rural state, but the 1920 census was the first to show more Hoosiers lived in cities than in the country. We import a lot of our gas now, no matter how much our cows might still generate.

Steel yourself

You can't get a better look Indiana contrast than to watch an industry from a beach. In this particular case it's the Dunes State Park beach, and from there it's easy to see the steel mills that grew in the Gary area. The steel industry has taken quite a hit since then, and it's not just the effects of Lake Michigan water that made the area part of the Rust Belt.

Chapter Eleven:
WHITE SHEETS AND POINTY HATS

I've always enjoyed making fun of the Ku Klux Klan. I've always enjoyed making fun of anyone who judges an entire group of individuals, any group, as all being the same. *Everyone* who does that is just stupid. (See what I did there?)

It's probably not my safest stance ever, but it would have been a whole lot less safe around a hundred years ago, when the Klan took over Indiana.

Yeah, you heard me right. I wish you hadn't.

The Indiana chapter of the KKK was founded in 1920. It had been more than fifty years since the end of the Civil War, but boy, those guys held a grudge. Although slaves had been freed, it was still a rough time to be black in America, and it wasn't getting any better.

Two years after the Klan came to Indiana, Hoosier D.C. Stephenson became the Grand Poohbah Racial Purity Guy for the national organization. The actual title is Grand Dragon, but I kind of like dragons and think the association is unfair. With that title Stephenson got control of the Klan in 23 states, and he promptly moved the organization's headquarters to his home state. Indianapolis became both the physical and moral—ahem, "moral"— capital of the national organization, which controlled the state capital through most of the 1920s.

Then, tragically and ironically, the Klan took over the party of Lincoln, with a slate of Republican candidates who swept the 1924 state elections. Now the Klan controlled the Indiana General Assembly, and put Edward L. Jackson in the governor's office.

He was, believe you me, absolutely no relation to Samuel L. Jackson.

The pointy-headed guys soon controlled the Indianapolis City Council, Board of school Commissioners, and the Marion County Board of County Commissioners. But Stephenson's goal was much, much bigger: control of the United States Congress, and then the White House.

The Klan hated all the usual people. To show they weren't just anti-color, they came out against Catholics, immigrants, and Jews, and fought against the establishment of parochial schools. Basically they hated anyone who didn't look and think exactly like them, a problem that continues with various groups to this day.

During Prohibition the KKK wanted strong punishment of bootleggers, what with the Klan being the law and order sort. They set up what they called a Horse Thief Detective Association to raid not horse thieves, but gambling and speakeasy operations. Why call it that, huh? Hiding behind a metaphorical sheet, were you? Huh? *Huh?*

Sorry.

The thing is, the Klan operation didn't bother to cooperate with actual law enforcement agencies or courts. In 1924, over Klan opposition, a Republican named Arthur Gillon was elected State Attorney General and came down hard on the Klan's raiding group. He reasoned surrendering individual freedoms and Constitutional rights was a slippery slope that would lead to centralized governments and tyranny.

In the next decade, events in Europe would prove him absolutely right.

Still, for now Gillon shouted into the wind. In Indiana, the Klan controlled both major political parties, and over half the seats in the General Assembly. Stephenson, who boasted "I am the law in Indiana", came close to doing there what Hitler would later do in Germany: take complete dictatorial control over the entire government, only without the spiffy Nazi uniforms. Seriously, white sheets?

Ah, but the faster those white sheets and hoods are cleaned and pressed, the faster they get stained and wrinkled. Not my best line ever.

Stephenson "invited" a young Indianapolis woman, Madge Oberholtzer, onto a train ride, where he raped and injured her, then abandoned her to die. You wouldn't think that would come from such a fine, upright kind of a guy, would you? At the end of 1925 he was convicted of the crime, but no prob—he had control of Governor Jackson.

But Jackson said, "I'm getting sick and tired of this mother bleeping Klan on this mother bleeping train". Wait, that's Samuel L. Jackson, and I think I got the line wrong.

When Jackson refused to pardon Stephenson, it all fell apart. There is no honor among thieves, but there's slightly more honor among thieves than there is among scumbag racists. An unpardoned Stephenson said, "Oh, yeah? Well, I need more inmates in this cell for bridge night." Then he started naming names.

Politicians keeled over like freshmen at a frat party. The Mayor of Indianapolis and numerous other officials ended up in jail. Governor Jackson only escaped that fate because, by the time they got around to him, the statute of limitations ran out. He served out the rest of his term disgraced and powerless.

Although they stuck around here and there, irritating as a sore toe but not nearly as useful, the Klan's power was broken in Indiana. The national organization disbanded in 1944, and the sheet manufacturing industry went into a depression.

Sadly their remnants are still around to this day, eyesores that stink up the place, like an old outhouse no one ever got around to tearing down. (Hey, I kind of like that—I should write it down.)

If there's a hopeful irony in all this, it's that the city of Indianapolis was later found to be one of the most racially integrated cities in the country. They didn't care about the color of your sheet, as long as you didn't wear it over your head.

Indianapolis is where Robert F. Kennedy happened to be on April 4, 1968, the day Martin Luther King Jr. was assassinated. Most of America's cities erupted into violent riots, and one could hardly blame Kennedy if he took the first plane out, or hid in his hotel room. It's not like he had a speech prepared, and even if he did—what could he say?

But Kennedy wasn't the type to hide under a bed.

Instead he delivered an off the cuff speech, not in some protected police barracks but in a poor inner-city neighborhood, to a mostly black crowd. He spoke of reconciliation, and it worked: Indianapolis was the only major American city that didn't suffer from wide-spread riots.

Bridging the Racial Divide
There didn't seem to be a good photo for the Klan section, until I thought of this one: the Martin Luther King Jr. Bridge in Fort Wayne. How many racists put extra miles on their cars to avoid crossing it? I don't know, but the idea made me smile.

Indiana Facts:
PRIMARY COLORS

Hoosiers will be stunned to learn their state used to matter in national elections.

No, seriously.

The primary system has morphed in such a way that the nominations for US President are usually settled by the time Indiana has its primary election in May. In addition, the state has become solidly red—Democratic presidential contenders might as well not bother to spend money here, and in the general election the Republican pick usually gets the nod. It's still up in the air from time to time, such as the Democratic primary fight in 2008, but mostly the national candidates don't bother. Campaign weary Hoosiers tend to breathe a sigh of relief.

But it wasn't always that way. Just the opposite: After the Civil War Indiana became a swing state, and often a deciding factor in the general election. The state echoed with rallies, parades, and speeches. Voter turnout?

You might want to sit down for this.

Voter turnout usually reached over 90%, and approached 100% in the elections of 1888 and 1896.

I *told* you to sit down.

Although outright fraud was surprisingly rare, it was common for party members to pay their supporters to vote, especially in rural areas. It wasn't unheard of for them to pay supporters of the other side *not* to vote. Yes, alcohol was also involved.

Indiana became so important that, between 1880 and 1924, a Hoosier was a member of the ticket for one party or another in all but one of the general elections. You might recall Benjamin Harrison, who won in 1888. 300,000 people came to hear him speak from his front porch during the campaign (a very nice front porch, I might add). Five Hoosiers have become Vice-President.

Now it seems as if Indiana no longer attends Electoral College ... or at least, we're no longer head of the class.

Chapter Twelve:
WAR! WHAT IS IT GOOD FOR?
(GETTING RID OF MURDEROUS DICTATORS, SAY IT AGAIN!)

Before the Great Depression we had a big war. After the Great Depression we had an even *bigger* war. It's depressing.

Most Hoosiers weren't all that interested in wars, what with all the killing and stuff. When World War I broke out the US was especially isolationist. We didn't want Irish coffee, we didn't want German beer, we didn't want Italian ice, and didn't we already decide about the British tea? Indiana's Democratic Senator John W. Kern wanted us to stay the heck out of it, and so did the Vice-President, Thomas R. Marshall. Woodrow Wilson campaigned for President on the platform of keeping us out of the war.

Hoosiers of Irish ancestry, who didn't exactly get along with our incipient British allies, opposed our involvement. So, as you might imagine, did German-Americans.

But German rulers didn't quite catch on to the fact that once we got riled, we got *really* riled. They went to unrestricted submarine warfare, which led to American deaths. Then they tried to get Mexico on their side, with the promise that Mexico could get the rest of their original country back. This despite the fact that the rest of original Mexico was in a nation not yet at war with Germany: The United States.

That didn't go over well with Mexico's northern neighbors.

In April, 1917, we promised to go Over There. This included units of the Indiana National Guard.

There was still some opposition to the war. Eugene V. Debs, a Socialist movement leader and perennial presidential candidate from Terra Haute, tried to get men to evade the draft, for instance. In turn, he was drafted into a federal prison, where I'm sure he socialized just fine. A few teachers suspected of disloyalty lost their jobs, and you couldn't find a German language class anywhere. You'd think we'd want to know what the enemy had to say about us.

But over there we went, with Indiana supplying 130,670 troops, most of them draftees. Over 3,000 of those died, but not all from bullets; most passed away from disease, including a flu epidemic that swept the world late in the war. To honor them, the state constructed what would become the Indiana World War Memorial.

We left the War to End All Wars and entered an area of progress and prosperity.

The Indiana World War Memorial
General John Pershing, commander of American forces in Europe, laid the cornerstone for the memorial in 1927, but funding problems kept the whole thing from being completed until 1965. If you get tired of looking at it from the outside— I didn't—you can go inside to the Indiana World War Memorial Military Museum, which if you're thorough will occupy you for several days. Indiana Jones would get lost in there.

Wait, What Happened To The Progress and Prosperity?

After the war, the Allies came down pretty hard on Germany. As if that wasn't bad enough the Great Depression hit Europe too, causing distress, unrest, and the rise of some pretty bad people. But what the heck, not our problem, right? Our economy sucked, too, so we had other things to worry about. In fact, why not turn our back on the rest of the world and lick our own wounds?

It worked so well last time.

Like last time, Germany made a major mistake when it came to dealing with the USA. Remember, Germany didn't bomb Pearl Harbor. (Spoiler alert: Japan did.) But Hitler had signed a treaty with Japan, so after the bombing Der Fuehrer declared war on America. I suppose he figured, how much trouble could we be? I mean, we were on the other side of a whole ocean.

By the way, Hitler fought in World War I. He should have known better.

This time, what with us being maliciously and deliberately attacked, the American people got behind the war effort. Even the Socialists wanted to help out, what with the Soviet Union also under attack thanks to Hitler not learning the lesson of Napoleon.

That lesson: Never attack Russia in the winter. Come on, Adolf. Seriously, you'd think the guy never picked up a history book.

Let's face it: Hitler, Mussolini, and Tojo were not the kind of people

I'd ship this

The USS LST 325 found a permanent home in Evansville after World War II service in the North Africa, Sicily, and Italy campaigns—not to mention hitting Omaha Beach on D-Day. The ship landed armored vehicles ("Landing Ship-Tank") and its crew is credited with rescuing over 700 men from a torpedoed troop transport.

Later it served in the Greek Navy before becoming a museum and memorial in Evansville—one of only two WWII LSTs preserved in the USA.

you'd want your daughter to bring home for dinner, and attacking American territory wasn't the best way to meet the family. Most church organizations, even the peaceful Quakers, considered WWII a just war, and volunteered their services where they could. Although the Mennonites and Brethren were pacifists, their young men provided non-military service to the country. In return the government, which messed with those churches a little during the First World War, generally left them alone this time.

Goshen College, which still operates in Indiana, was set up to train those pacifists for unpaid Civilian Public Service jobs, which included work in hospitals—and many of the civilians who took those jobs were women. Although not eligible for the draft, they wanted to do their part anyway, which just goes to show a determined woman can beat up Hitler anytime (and wouldn't it have been great to see that?).

Elsewhere, women served in the Red Cross, often in dangerous areas, and suffered casualties. If we'd let them fight, the whole thing would have been over by Mother's Day, 1944.

On the home front, factories mobilized all over the state, which ended any thought of an economic depression. I already mentioned Indiana's state plane, the P-47 fighter, which was made in Evansville by Republic Aviation. Hoosier steel went into tanks, battleships, and submarines, and military bases turned out trained manpower.

We sent almost 400,000 Hoosiers to fight in WWII, and around 10,000 never came back. 17,000 more were wounded, in all theaters of the war. Much can be learned about them at the World War Memorial in Indianapolis.

Among famous Indiana residents who went to war was Ernie Pyle, a correspondent who became a favorite of the soldiers he served with. Ernie said:

"If I can just see the European war out, I think I might feel justified in quitting the war."

But when the war in Europe ended, Ernie couldn't leave the front line GIs he'd come to love. He traveled on over to the Asian theater of operation, where he was killed by Japanese machine gun fire.

"At last we are in it up to our necks."

Two of Ernie Pyle's books are on display at the National Military History Center in Auburn. A statue of Pyle, a Hoosier journalist killed at Okinawa during World War II, stands at Franklin Hall, the Media School at Indiana University.

Indiana Facts:

There's no shortage of famous people from Indiana. However, "famous" is relative, and I don't mean when only your relatives know you.

For instance, if you're a Hoosier and have an interest in literature, you instantly recognize the name Gene Stratton-Porter. She's as famous an author as William Forsyth, James Whitcomb Riley, Kurt Vonnegut, Jr., or Lew Wallace.

Okay, you may not have heard of them, either. Maybe instead you're a sports fan, which means *Space Jam* star Larry Bird (who also plays basketball), Don Mattingly, Knute Rockne, Oscar Robertson, or Tony Stewart might be familiar to you. I'm not a sports fan, and even I've heard of some of them.

Rockne, you kidding me? He was a coach, or something. Come on, *Knute Rockne, All-American*! "Win one for the Gipper"? That guy. Just trust me on this.

By the way, Bird became known as the "Hick from French Lick". There are worse nicknames, but Bird actually came from an adjoining town, West Baden. A resort hotel in West Baden boasted the largest free spanning dome in the world from 1902 to 1913, so it wasn't so very hick.

Okay, I'm more familiar with Stratton-Porter than the sports people. Still—they're all Hoosiers.

Stratton-Porter was an author and photographer at a time when being either seemed unwomanly, whatever that means. She was a naturalist who also formed her own movie studio and production company, all while wearing corsets and swooning. I made that last part up, probably. But one of her novels got turned into a movie *four times*, and most writers could only hope for such a deal. *sob*

Vonnegut made out pretty good, too.

Lots of entertainers start out in Indiana, even if they end up somewhere else. You're probably familiar with David Letterman. I'm not sure what talent is required for a talk show host. It isn't exactly acting, it isn't exactly comedian, it's not quite song and dance man. Or maybe it is, I seldom watched his show— don't tell.

Indiana has entertainers:

James Dean of Marion, who did the brooding rebel without a cause thing in movies such as *Rebel Without a Cause*.

Avery Brooks of Evansville, one of the *Star Trek* captains.

Ron Glass of Evansville, from the TV shows *Barney Miller* and my favorite, *Firefly*.

Axle Rose of Lafayette, a fan of both Guns N' Roses.

David Lee Roth of Bloomington, and Mick Mars of Terre Haute, both later of Mötley Crüe ... we really rock in the Hoosier state.

Vivica A. Fox of Naptown, who starred in a lot of good movies and also *Sharknado 2: The Second One*.

Brendan Fraser, also of Naptown, who fought mummies and swung through the trees in various movies, although not at the same time.

You'll find the Huntington County Courthouse in Huntington County—I checked

I included this photo mostly because one Huntington County celebrity is J. Edward Roush. A U.S. Representative, he's known as the "Father of 911 Emergency System". After two decades as an emergency dispatcher, I can appreciate that.

But the courthouse is cool, too.

Mike Epps of Naptown, a comedian ...

Wait.

Naptown?

Okay, research done. It's a nickname for Indianapolis, started by jazz musicians in the 30s because they got tired of hitting all the syllables in "Indianapolis". What, they never heard of "Indy"? Apparently some musicians and other people began to use the phrase again after the turn of this century.

Hey, we learned something new today! Ahem. Where were we?

Oh, yes. Next is Karl Malden of Gary, an actor who never left home without his American Express Card.

Jim Davis of Fairmount and his cartoon kitty, Garfield.

Strother Martin of Kokomo, another actor and all around cool guy.

Steve McQueen, Beech Grove—forget what I said about anyone else being cool.

Carole Lombard of Fort Wayne, glamorous actress who died in a plane crash during World War II.

Shelley Long of Fort Wayne, who famously quit the TV show *Cheers* at the height of its popularity.

Florence Henderson, everyone's favorite mother on *The Brady Bunch*. When that show got turned into a movie years later, the mom's part was taken over by ... Shelley Long.

Hoagy Carmichael of Bloomington, who wrote great songs in addition to inventing a wonderful sandwich.

Michael Jackson (and family) of Gary—you've probably heard of them.

John Cougar Mellencamp of Seymour, singer and last known wild cougar in the state.

Cole Porter of Peru, who wrote the songs that made a generation swoon.

Red Skelton of Vincennes, comedian and clown with a long, celebrated career of making people laugh.

Forrest Tucker of Plainfield, comic actor who I remember best in *F-Troop*.

James McCracken of Gary, considered one of the best opera singers ever. He was so good audiences at the Met, impatient for him to perform, would shout, "Release McCracken!"

We also have some miscellaneous people of fair to moderate fame:

For instance, Bill Blass of Fort Wayne, who's a famous fashion designer. Rumor has it he's the guy who legitimized the t-shirt in high fashion.

Virgil Grissom of Mitchell, an astronaut who tragically died in the Apollo 1 fire.

Earl Butz of my hometown, Albion, who became U.S. Secretary of Agriculture.

Jeff Gordon of Pittsboro and Tony Stewart of Columbus, who drive cars and stuff.

Ford Frick of Wawaka, Commissioner of Major League Baseball.

Amelia Earhart, an aviator who left Indiana and never looked back. Is it too soon for a getting lost joke?

Jimmy Hoffa of Brazil, labor leader and, according to rumor, anchorman for the end zone at Lucas Oil Stadium.

Harlan David Sanders, a farmer, salesman, steamboat pilot, and railroad fireman who later established a chicken café and got promoted to Colonel.

Wilbur Wright of Millville, who ran an Ohio bicycle shop with his brother and later invented flying.

John Dillinger of Indianapolis, who robbed a bank or two in a long career broken only by a nine year vacation behind bars, and later by getting shot.

And my favorite: Orville Redenbacher of Brazil. His company claims to produce 90% of all the popcorn. In the world. *That's* where all the Indiana corn goes.

This is, believe me, only a partial list of Hoosier celebrities and accomplished people. (Being one of those doesn't guarantee the other, of course.) It's a representative sample, I think ... and if not, to be honest, my typing fingers were getting tired.

One more kind of related thing, though: Daniel Boone is generally remembered for his adventures further east. In fact, I used to travel the Daniel Boone Parkway to get to my grandparents' Kentucky home. But Daniel and his brother Squire visited southern Indiana, where Squire settled and later died. Squire Boone's bones (well, most of them) are in a coffin that can be seen on a cave tour near where he and his brother once hid from Native Americans. The cave is known, of course, as the Squire Boone Caverns.

So ... We're deep in a dark cavern with a dead body?

Nothing fuels discovery like running for your life. Squire and Daniel Boone were hiding from Indians when in 1790 they discovered what would become the Squire Boone Caverns. Later Squire, ignoring his history of being shot and tomahawked, came back to the future Harrison County for good.

In 1815, at age 70, Squire was buried in a small pit cave, as he requested (he died first). But a hundred years later relic hunters began stealing parts of his coffin and even some bones—who does that? In 1973 his remaining bones were put in a new coffin, in a part of the caverns seen during regular tours. Seriously, stealing bones?

Chapter Thirteen

GENTLEMEN, START YOUR AUTOMOTIVE MANUFACTURING COMPANIES

On July 4th, 1894, Elwood Haynes decided fireworks and fancy speeches weren't enough of a revolutionary celebration for him. So he built a car.

These days nobody just goes off and builds a car all by themselves. In those days, a lot of people had never even seen a car. Undaunted, and aware that all those cool car names were just out there for the taking, Haynes opened the Elwood-Haynes Auto Company after two years of development.

First he considering a steam engine to power his car, but it occurred to him mounting a furnace and a very hot pressurized container on a moving vehicle might not be the safest plan ever. Then he thought about electricity, but there were no decent batteries, and his five mile long extension cord proved impractical. Finally he sent off to the Stintz Gas Engine Company for a one-horsepower gasoline engine which was probably, and ironically, delivered by train and horse drawn wagon.

He fired up the engine on a carriage he'd built in his kitchen. Yeah, I know. The thing vibrated so badly it damaged the carriage and his kitchen floor, and filled his house with smoke.

That's when his wife said, "Why don't you just build your own little shop for these experiments? Or else?"

But in the end it worked, traveling a mile and a half at 7 miles per hour. Really, how much faster do you need to go? It was the second gas powered automobile to be successfully road tested in the US—curse that Charles Duryeah of Massachusetts! It beat Henry Ford by two years, although you have to figure he got the last laugh.

Haynes also got involved in what's thought to be the first car accident—ever. This happened in Chicago, so it was far from the last one.

By then roads crisscrossed Indiana (Crossroads, yada yada), all ready for the first stop light, the first speeding ticket, the first traffic jam—all the extras that make commuting worthwhile. Indianapolis—where, after all, the crossroads crossed—based automotive companies sprung up like, well, metal springs.

In fact, in the early 20th Century more than 250 manufacturers made automobiles in Indiana. Duesenberg, Marmon, National, and Stutz were just a few new companies in the capital itself, while many smaller cities saw their own companies come and go. Mostly, they went. But hey, they went fast. By 1909 Indiana was number two in car production, and you can guess what border state made number one.

I wouldn't brake-check this guy

Yes, Hoosiers love their guns. But I'm betting this Jeep and its accompanying 50 caliber machine gun, seen at the Indiana World War Memorial Plaza, means one of two things: Either there was a display of military equipment going on (there was), or Indianapolis traffic really is as bad as they say (it is).

The difference was Indiana car makers were craftsmen, who turned out the cars piece by piece, one at a time. That made them quality products, but expensive. Up in Michigan they perfected mass production techniques, which would eventually take over like machines in a science fiction thriller.

Come With Me If You Want a New Car

Let's go back in time to John Conner. No, not the John Conner who led a worldwide revolt against the rise of the machines—he never founded a town. Our John Conner was a fur trader, who named a new town after himself in 1808. Probably for the best: It could have been Furville. Instead, the east-central Indiana city of Connersville later got the nickname "Little Detroit", and not in a bad way.

Carmakers including Auburn, Cord, Duesenberg, and several others had facilities in Connersville. (Now you can visit the Auburn-Cord-Duesenberg Museum in Auburn. So far as I know, there is no town named Cord.) Per capita, Connersville was once the automotive manufacturing capital of the world. In your face, Detroit.

One specific company, Auburn Automobile, became the 13th biggest car manufacturer in the country in 1931. At the time they built not only the Cord, which sadly had no town named after it, but also the luxury Duesenbergs and the less luxurious, but very familiar, Checker Cabs.

Meanwhile a guy named Harry Clayton Stutz got an idea to launch the Ideal Car Company in 1911, after his car did well in the first of what would become a familiar car race. Stutz made the famous Bearcat, and came up with the transaxle for front wheel drive cars. The transaxle was pretty cool, and revolutionized front wheel drive. No, I don't know what it does.

At the time fire departments across the country realized the days of horse-drawn fire apparatus were numbered, so demand rose for gasoline powered fire trucks ... especially as the number of car fires increased. Stutz moved on to form the HCS Motor Car Company and also the Stutz Fire Engine Company, which made ... you know.

In the end it wasn't his cars and trucks that put the brakes on Stutz—it was the Great Depression.

As for the building where Stutz made his cars, it got bought by Eli Lilly, who made the drugs people now take when they get stressed out by traffic. It became the Stutz Business Center, and that was the end of it.

Or so it seemed. Stutz luxury cars started rolling out again in the late sixties, until 1988. Another thousand or so were turned out, mostly to unknown buyers such as Elvis Presley and Evil Knievel.

Calm Down, not That Kind of Model

The largest Indiana carmaker was Studebaker, which started out in 1901, and kept on going until 1963. It wasn't the only one, though:

The Cole Motor Car Company of Indianapolis operated from 1909 to 1925, and provided the first Presidential automobile in US history. That was for William Taft, so it can be assumed they strengthened the suspension.

The Marmon Motor Car Company started out making flour mill machinery. You have to wonder why they named it a motor car company. Their luxury car was the Marmon, a much more attractive name than the Flourmill, and they made it until 1933.

The Stutz Motor Company, which we've already heard about, was taken over by a Bethlehem Steel tycoon, Charles M. Schwab. This explains why Mr. Stutz moved on to fire trucks, which are way cooler anyway.

Duesenberg was a luxury car for luxury people, and I wouldn't be surprised if Schwab owned one. Although they were thought to be the finest automobiles ever built, the Great Depression had no appetite for finery.

George Milburn, of Mishawaka, made electric cars—pretty unusual at a time when batteries weren't so hot. He supplied some of his Milburns to the Secret Service in 1918, as those guys were juiced to keep an eye on Woodrow Wilson. Milburn moved his operation to Toledo (in not-Indiana) after Mishawaka officials refused to run a railroad line to his factory.

Not so famous was the Moore Car out of Indianapolis, which was a car, sort of, when its outriggers were out. It looked more like a motorcycle with training wheels, which could be raised and lowered. W.G. Moore insisted it was *not* a motorcycle ... just a really inexpensive car. It stuck around until 1919. You would think, considering it had no passenger compartment, the

The Marmon Wasp

If you want the attention of a Hoosier car lover, blow through town in the 1911 Marmon Wasp, shown here hitting Albion on all cylinders. Engineer Ray Harroun assembled the six-cylinder Wasp from stock Marmon engine components, and raced it in the 1911 Indianapolis 500—the very first one. He also won, thanks partially to his odd and innovative rear-view mirror.

first Indiana winter would do it in.

Then came Milton O. Reeves of Columbus (Indiana, not that other place). He had kind of the opposite idea, after experiencing one too many flat tires. If four wheels were good, why not eight wheels?

Reeves brought his caterpillar car (catercar?) to the first Indianapolis 500 in 1911, and it went over well. With so many tires, it would go over anything well, wouldn't it? But it never went into mass production, although the Reeves Company made engines until Cummings Machine Company bought them out in 1914.

Ah, yes, the Indianapolis 500. We should probably mention that at some point, shouldn't we?

Have I Got a Deal for You

But first we should mention that with all good comes the bad. With the new automobile industry, for instance, came ... car salesmen.

A guy named Carl Fisher—you'll hear his name later—ran an Indianapolis bicycle repair shop in the 1890s. But in that town, all everyone wanted to talk about was that newfangled automobile. Fisher was soon to make a fortune manufacturing car headlamps with a guy named James Allison, whose name would come to be associated with racing. Fisher also opened one of the first automobile dealerships in the nation, where he sold Packards, Stutzes, and Oldsmobiles.

Even back then, selling cars was all about stunts and making noise. So, Fisher hooked a car chassis to a hot air balloon and floated it over the city.

"Look, Ma—it's one of them newfangled car-planes."

Fisher also convinced private interests to build an improved highway, a road that could take drivers all the way from New York to San Francisco. They started it in 1913 and it became a huge hit, paving the way (ahem) for the Interstate Highway system. That road became known as the Lincoln Highway, and you don't get much more historic.

Oh, and Fisher also partnered to build a proving ground, where auto manufacturers could showcase their new cars. He called it the Indianapolis Motor Speedway.

Indiana Facts:

LIGHTS ... CAMERA ... HOOSIERS!

There are two kinds of movies and TV shows when it comes to a connection with the Hoosier state: Those filmed in Indiana, and those about Indiana. The perfect movie, of course, claims both honors.

Maybe the most perfect Hoosier movie has the perfect name: *Hoosiers*. It tells the true story of tiny Milan High School, which won a basketball championship against an array of much bigger teams. Even I loved this movie, and I despise basketball with every fiber of my athletic supporter.

For TV shows, there's *Eerie, Indiana*, which is not connected to the real town of Erie, Indiana. Still, eerily, it's set in Eerie, in Indiana.

Do Not Adjust Your Set

(Shows set in Indiana)

Eerie, Indiana only lasted one very odd season, along with another rebooted season. Other Indiana-based TV shows did better ... and others, not so much. The big question for Hoosiers is often whether anyone involved in making a show ever actually set foot in Indiana ... usually the answer is no.

With *The Middle*, the answer is a resounding "yes". Set in the fictional town of Orson in southern Indiana, this sitcom is about a dysfunctional Midwestern family. It either has Hoosiers in the crew, or is the best researched show in television history. (I'm told Orson is based on Jasper, Indiana.)

Parks and Recreation was a seven year sitcom about the parks department in Pawnee, Indiana. Although Pawnee doesn't exist, they had the right idea in naming it after a Native American tribe.

Armed and Famous is a reality show in which celebrities become reserve police officers for the Muncie Police Department. I eschew this type of reality TV, so I've never seen this. "Eschew" is a Latin word meaning "hate with a fiery passion".

The Fugitive: Is this cheating? The story starts in Stafford, Indiana, but once the main character goes on the run from the charge of killing his wife, it goes all over the country. (Spoiler alert: He's not guilty.)

I suppose the opposite of that would be *Supernatural,* which has had its characters visit real Indiana towns.

Garfield and Friends: This cartoon was based on Hoosier Jim Davis' characters and ran for seven seasons (!). Over the course of the show it's revealed the main characters live at 357 Shady Grove Lane, Muncie, IN 47305. Yes, 47305 is Muncie's Zip Code, and yes, Davis and his production company are from Muncie.

One Day at a Time ran for nine years, and featured a single mom and her two teenage daughters in Indianapolis. My recollection is it could have been set in any American city, and that Valerie Bertinelli was hot.

The Jeff Foxworthy Show—I don't have to tell you who starred, right?— was set in Bloomington its first season, then moved to a different network and to Georgia in its second. The audience, enraged at the locale shift, insisted the show either head back north or shut down, so a fearful NBC cancelled it.

By the way, a son on that show was played by young Haley Joel Osment. The year before, Osment played the little kid in *Thunder Alley,* another two season sitcom also set in Indiana. The outside of the fictitious garage/home in that series was filmed in Kimmell, in Noble County. Just the outside, nothing else.

There were a few others, forgettable and forgotten, such as The 5 Mrs. Buchanans, Glory Daze, Hang Time, Maggie Winters, Men Behaving Badly, and Thrill Seekers, as well as a version of the movie Breaking Away.

If you need a flyover state, why not pick this one?

There was also a little known Saturday morning show called *Good Morning, Miss Bliss,* set in an Indianapolis middle school. After one season it was retooled, Miss Bliss got pink slipped, the kids all moved to California, and the show was retitled *Saved by the Bell.*

Shows Filmed in Indiana

There were no TV shows filmed in Indiana, if you don't include *Armed and Famous.* Well, none I could find, and I'm way too lazy to make it an issue. There are a couple that had exteriors shot in Indiana, but were otherwise filmed elsewhere, which is cheating.

"Roseanne" house, Terra Haute

Although the sitcom "Roseanne" was set in Lanford, Illinois, the family home exterior is in an Evansville neighborhood that looks just like the one you'd picture the Conner clan inhabiting. The show ended in 1997, but the house looks pretty much the same; come to think of it, so does Roseanne.

Let's Go To the Movies

(Movies Filmed in Indiana)

The 2010 version of *A Nightmare on Elm Street* was filmed partially in Gary, but they went to Illinois too, searching for locations "old and decaying". Not complimentary, but what the heck—they brought money.

I don't know how much of Gary remained after *Transformers: Dark of the Moon* was shot there.

Rain Man was short partially in Franklin County, and starred Tom Cruise as someone who could act and Dustin Hoffman as someone who really can act.

It's only Fair Play

When my fire department (Albion) was formed in 1888, what's now called the Fair Play Fire Company No. 1 was already almost sixty years old. The Union Volunteer Fire Company was organized to protect the city of Madison in 1830; after a failed experiment with a paid department, the volunteers reorganized as Fair Play. It's only fair to declare them the oldest volunteer fire company in Indiana.

Of course Madison, along the Ohio River, was formed way back in 1810—before the state even existed—so their fire protection had a head start. In 1888 (to celebrate the Albion Fire Department's founding, no doubt), Fair Play moved into their present building, an 1875 former streetcar barn. The volunteers added the 3 ½ story hose drying tower, which is topped by the department's mascot, "Little Jimmy".

Natural Born Killers, a movie that's hard to sit through, was partially filmed in the Hammond City Courtroom.

Winning, a 1969 Paul Newman flick totally unrelated to Charlie Sheen, just about had to be filmed in Indy: It's all about the Indianapolis 500. So, they shot it there. These days it would be a giant green screen with CGI added later.

Speaking of Charlie Sheen, he did come to Indiana for *Eight Men Out*, shot in Indy and Evansville.

Some Came Running is notable because it brought Frank Sinatra, Dean Martin, and Shirley McLaine to Madison, Indiana, an elderly (by Indiana standards) town along the Ohio River. It's set in a town called Parkman, but I'm not sure if that's supposed to be in the Hoosier state. Why not?

Let's Hear From the Movies

(Movies Set In Indiana)

Parts of *Close Encounters of the Third Kind* take place in and around Muncie and Indianapolis ... and other parts of the universe. You'd think Spielberg could have dropped by with a camera.

A Christmas Story is one of my favorite Christmas movies, because it reminds me so much of my own childhood—up to and including a beloved BB gun. It was based on a book by Indiana author Jean Shepherd and is set in a fictionalized version of Hammond.

It was filmed in Cleveland. Except for the parts filmed in Ontario.

Madison: A racer struggles to win a power boat race in Madison, Indiana. How I missed this movie I don't know, but if it wasn't actually filmed in Madison there's no justice in the world.

Tecumseh is about real life Native American leader Tecumseh, who died in the War of 1812 while fighting with the British. It was made during the Cold War by a communist state-owned East German studio, and I must once more point out I am *not* making this up. As you might imagine, it was a bit critical of Indiana Governor Harrison and the USA in general.

Abraham Lincoln: Vampire Hunter accurately sets Abe Lincoln in Indiana during his youth. Past that, rumor is it's not all that historically accurate.

Irreconcilable Differences starts in Indiana, and moves on to little Drew Barrymore suing her parents for divorce. Fort Wayne's Shelly Long comes home as the mom—sort of.

Let's Go To and From the Movies

(What's Filmed Here, Stays Here)

You don't get more Hoosier than *Hoosiers*. Although they took liberties with the story of the 1954 Milan High School basketball triumph, it's still pretty darned Hoosier-ish. In fact, the announcer at the final game is Hilliard Gates, the same Indiana sports announcer who called the real game. It even has an awesome, evocative score by Jerry Goldsmith that just screamed Indiana ... played by the Hungarian State Opera orchestra of Budapest.

Hoosiers has the underdog story, the basketball, even the name ... it's quintessential. At least that's my assumption, until I look up what quintessential means.

Just the same, it could get competition from the 1979 movie *Breaking Away*, another sports film. It's about working class friends in Bloomington, Indiana who get involved in the annual Indiana University Little 500 bike race, even though they seem destined to work in the Indiana limestone industry.

All of this is real stuff in real places; we've already discussed Indiana limestone. It was all filmed around Bloomington and the IU campus, and after winning an Oscar it became a TV series.

It also inspired a Bollywood film, Jo Jeeta Wohi Sikandar. That translates roughly to Get the Powder, These Bike Seats Are Killing Me.

I have no answer for why sports films and Indiana seem so intertwined, but much of *A League of Their Own* was filmed in Evansville and other areas of southwest Indiana.

On a not unrelated not, the football film *Rudy* was filmed partially in Indiana, which makes sense as it concerns a player trying to get into Notre Dame University. This movie also has a Jerry Goldsmith score, so it has to be good.

No, no: Even Milan High School was bigger than this
There's been a school at this Noble County location since 1845 ... not with the same students. The 1915 Stanley Schoolhouse was named after Henry Stanley, who turned 500 acres of wilderness into farmland; later much of that land was turned back into wilderness, becoming Chain O' Lakes State Park. Similarly, the building was turned back into a schoolhouse, to show visitors what the experience of the time was like. Believe me, there wasn't a lot of e-learning.

Chapter Fourteen

I TOOK MY CHEVY TO THE LEVY AND RACED IT AROUND IN CIRCLES

To say I'm not a huge sports fan is an understatement: In my house, no one knows the difference between basketball shorts and bicycle shorts. But there are two sports events I try to catch every year: The Super Bowl (for the commercials) and the only event that's required watching for Hoosiers by vote of the Indiana State Legislature.

That's right: The Indianapolis 500, also known as the Greatest Spectacle in Racing. The 500 is such a big deal it's often called simply The 500. It's part of a racing league that's actually called Indy Car Racing.

And it doesn't take place in Indianapolis.

Honestly, the race hasn't been the same since Jim Nabors retired, but it still has milk.

Something is Fisher in the State of Indiana

We already know Carl Fisher started out with a bicycle repair shop in Indianapolis, then opened one of the first auto dealerships in the country. After Fisher got rich making "Presto-O-Lite", a gas fueled headlamp for early cars, he sold the company to Union Carbide for nine million dollars.

Well, what does one do with nine million bucks in the early 1900s, in an area exploding with automobile manufacturers? That's right: Taco stands.

Kidding! And good thing too, because tacos were not yet popular in Indiana. Maybe Fisher knew the walking taco would someday become popular, but he was all about driving. (Walking tacos are a lot like sitting still tacos, but in a bag. You don't want a running taco.)

Automobiles were still largely experimental in those days, and manufacturers needed to test their products at a location that didn't involve running over pedestrians. So Fisher got the idea of a proving ground: A place where automakers could showcase, and test out, their latest models. And what better way to test a car than to race it against other cars?

The plan: Build a motor speedway in French Lick. But people just laughed at that. Also nobody liked their proposed name, the Indiana Motor Parkway Grounds.

So in 1909 Fisher and three partners built the Indianapolis Motor Speedway, five miles northwest of Indianapolis. Not *in* Indianapolis. Okay, a little misleading, but keep in mind: The guy was a car salesman.

The idea turned into a total flop.

Well, the first race, in June, 1909, went over well. In fact, it went over literally: It was a gas balloon race, and one of the nine starters was Fisher himself. The winner landed in Alabama, 382 miles away. But the road racing didn't work out so well, and an August, 1909 motorcycle race proved a disaster.

You see, they paved the two and a half mile oval with crushed stone, and have you ever tried to drive in fast circles on gravel? No, don't tell me, unless you're sure the statute of limitations is up. Tar was applied, but tar over crushed stone didn't do the trick.

So instead, Fisher had the Speedway paved with bricks. 3.2 *million* bricks. The first race on the brickyard was a 200 mile contest, won by Ray Harroun driving an Indiana-made Marmon. But for the shorter races attendance fell, and the idea grew to have a long endurance race—say, 500 miles. The first Indianapolis 500 was off, just in time for Memorial Day, 1911.

Only it was called the International 500-Mile Sweepstakes Race back then. That didn't change until 1981, and now it's formally the "Whatever-th Indianapolis 500-Mile Race". On the Borg-Warner Trophy, which the winner gets while slurping milk, it says only "Indianapolis 500-Mile Race", because who wants to carve a date in every year? But this is Indiana, and we call it what we want.

Fisher had a town named after him, north of Indianapolis, which is why the Speedway is sometimes known as the Greatest Spectacle in Fish Tacos. I'm kidding—the Speedway is actually in a town called, yes, Speedway, which is now surrounded by Indianapolis. So technically it should be the Speedway Motor Speedway.

There *is* a town called Fishers north of Indy, platted as Fisher's Switch way back in 1872 by Salathial Fisher, who had nothing to do with cars or tacos. Which is too bad, because then I could make a pun about Fisher tacos.

As for our Fisher, after pioneering a coast to coast highway (the Lincoln Highway), he started pushing for the Dixie Highway. It would run from Indianapolis to Florida, where Fisher wanted to turn a quiet little Florida village into a tourist destination. It just so happened Fisher had a resort in tiny Miami Beach, which saw a 440 percent growth in the early 20s.

Fisher always thought ahead.

The Indianapolis Motor Speedway

It's easy to find spectacular images of the place where the Greatest Spectacle in Racing happens. But if you happen to be just driving down the road in Speedway, maybe paying more attention to your GPS or cell phone than your location, you might be surprised to happen upon—this. I thought it might be interesting to see a more average spot around the highest capacity sports venue in the world, which covers over 559 acres and is big enough to hold a golf course. Oh, wait ... it does hold a golf course.

Turn Left. Okay, Just Keep Turning Left

40 cars started in that first race on May 30, 1911, which featured guest judge Henry Ford. Harroun, still in a Marmon, started the race with an innovation called a rear view mirror. He was the only racer without a riding mechanic, a guy whose main job was to check the car's oil pressure and warn the driver about oncoming traffic. Mirrors were way cheaper.

Harroun left everyone else in that mirror and won the first 500 ... depending on who you ask. Another racer, Ralph Mulford, made an official protest, which is like an unofficial protest only without foot stamping.

In Mulford's defense, a horrible multi-car accident 13 laps in threw scoring off for the rest of the race. Instant replay? No TV. Replaying the radio did no good at all.

Harroun reached the astounding speed of 74.59 miles per hour, which these days will get you run over on the interstate.

Someone must have agreed with Mulford, because next year riding mechanics became mandatory. The second race was also won by an Indiana-made car: a National, driven by American Joe Dawson. But by then European auto makers caught on, and they won the race for the next seven years. Ever since then, you see a lot of un-American drivers in the Indy 500. Um, I mean drivers who aren't from America.

Not that the audience seems to mind—about 300,000 attend the race these days.

The field starts with 33 cars now, but that's the only place where numbers have gone down. The Indianapolis 500 is believed to be the largest one day sporting event in the world, in the world's largest sports facility. The winner gets over $2.5 million, which he no longer has to share with a riding mechanic, so you can see how careful he is in using that mirror.

There are even events within the event: In 1927 the Purdue All-American Marching Band performed on the track, and they've been there ever since. Not during the race, of course, although that would certainly add excitement.

In 1946 an opera star, James Melton, showed up. Not to sing—he was just an operatic racing fan. But Speedway President Tony Hulman noticed him there and asked for a performance, which began the tradition of singing "Back Home Again in Indiana" before the race. Jim Nabors, best known as nasally-voice Gomer Pyle on TV, surprised audiences from 1972 until 2014 with his deep bass version of the song. In 2015 the group Straight No Chaser, which originated at Indiana University, got the job. Music! At a car race! Who says Hoosiers don't have culture?

Girls Have Car Cooties

Females were not welcome at the Indianapolis 500, unless they brought beer and sat in the grandstands. Even female news reporters weren't allowed in until 1971, which may seem silly, but that's only because it was silly. Then, in 1977, Janet Guthrie showed up to drive. You could say she was slumming it, since she was an aerospace engineer, but she didn't really care what you thought. Her car developed engine troubles and didn't finish, but it sure started something—nine women qualified in the years after. You might say she ... paved the way.

Sarah Fisher—and there's a name that brings it full circle, although as far as I know she's not related—competed nine times, and Danica Patrick became the first woman to take the lead, in addition to her third place finish in 2009.

So when somebody says you drive like a woman … look out.

Oh, and the milk! In 1933 Louis Meyer won his second Indy 500 race. Having just driven 500 miles he was naturally thirsty, and asked for a glass of—not milk, but buttermilk.

Ew.

When he won again in 1936 they didn't have a glass, so somebody handed him a bottle of buttermilk. (Ew.) He was caught on camera drinking from the bottle while he held up three fingers, because the V for victory sign means something else in England. (No, it was because he'd won three times.)

A local dairy company thought … hey, publicity! They offered a bottle of milk to all future winners, unaware Meyer's milk tasted extra buttery. (Ew.)

Ironically, drivers today can get it only whole, 2%, and skim, so no ew buttermilk. In 1993 winner Emerson Fittipaldi caused another kind of fit when he drank orange juice instead of milk … turns out he owned an orange grove.

Maybe Fittipaldi was lactose intolerant? And that explains why the drink comes *after* the race—you don't want to be the gassy driver stuck in a tiny race car for 500 miles.

So, the spectacle continues, and you can see it in the comfort of your own home, live. You might be surprised to learn it wasn't always that way: The race was on tape delay until 1986, when ABC went live for the first time (except for the local Indianapolis affiliate). In fact, in the late 60s the race didn't get televised until an edited version came out a week later, on the TV show Wide World of Sports. These days, even practice and qualifications are streamed live over the internet.

A side note: One early racer was famed WWI flying ace Eddie Rickenbacker, who only managed to finish once and overall didn't do so well. Later he got his revenge by becoming president of the Speedway, which he led through the Great Depression.

As another side note, on the Centennial of the first Indy 500, the Speedway celebrated its Centennial. See how that works?

Indiana Facts:
HOOSIER HYSTERICAL

You'd think it would be impossible to write a book about Indiana without mentioning basketball. But I'm going to try.

And In Other Sports …

Still, it's impossible to talk about Indiana without discussing sports. I mean—Indy 500, and all. But it's not all about big team sports. Well, not *all*.

For instance, for all the fuss about swimmer Michael Phelps and his record 8 Olympic medals, he's not the record holder in most of those events. That honor belongs to Mark Spitz—I'll pause while you laugh at his name.

Spitz won 7 gold medals, way back in the 1972 Olympics. Although Phelps is now ahead of him in the medal count, to this day Spitz still has the world record for all seven of his events.

But yeah, it's largely about racing and teams.

Okay, Fine.

Indiana has produced more NBA players per capita than any other state, and Muncie the most per capita of any other city (two other Hoosier cities are in the top ten). For those of you who, like me, would rather avoid the issue and be ignorant, NBA stands for the National Basketball Association.

sigh

In 1925 a guy names James Naismith sat in on the Indiana high school basketball finals, and wrote, "Basketball really had its origin in Indiana, which remains the center of the sport".

This despite the fact that basketball was developed in Massachusetts in 1891—by James Naismith. But at least on the high school level basketball seems to have started here, and you can't argue with its inventor.

Apparently we even have a pro basketball team in Indianapolis, called the Fakers, or Facers, or Pacers, or something. They came along in 1967, and took their name partially from the state's history with Indianapolis 500 pace cars and, a little more obscurely, the harness racing industries.

Oh. *Pacers*. I get it.

Any Given Friday

High school sports buffs, when not buffing about basketball, go nuts over football. As a high school student I was more of a fan of girls' sports, because ... girls. But we now have a professional football team too, after the Baltimore Colts decided Maryland weather just wasn't cold and miserable enough for them during playoff season.

Not to be outdone, other sports have pro or semi-pro teams in Indiana, the difference being that semi-pro teams live out of big trucks.

The Indy Eleven is a Soccer team that consists, I assume, of eleven players, or possibly eight players and three cheerleaders.

The Indianapolis Indians Triple A baseball team has, I again assume, by now bowed to pressure and become the Indianapolis Politically Corrects.

The Indiana Fever is a pro women's basketball team and no, I still won't watch.

The Indy Fuel, Evansville IceMen, and Fort Wayne Komets are ice hockey teams. The next ice age could start at any moment, and won't the rest of us be sorry.

The Fort Wayne Tin Caps used to be the Wizards, a much better name for a baseball team. But hey—Johnny Appleseed had his cookery headwear and Fort Wayne connection, so—Tin Caps. I get it.

The Fort Wayne Mad Ants have a similar naming gyration. Mad Anthony Wayne ... Mad Ants. Again, I get it, but an insect ant seems to be their logo. They couldn't find a blue uniform?

If I'm missing anyone ... I don't care.

So, Why an Oaken Bucket?

In Indiana, students go to college for two reasons: Sports, and they can't remember the other one.

Concentrating on sports seems to do the trick, though. The appropriately named Indiana Hoosiers have won five NCAA national championships and 21 Big Ten Conference championships, while the Purdue

Boilermakers have one and 22 of something similar. I don't know what that means, but it sounds impressive.

Up in the northwest, where there's nothing else to do except add extra insulation to the house, the Notre Dame Fighting Irish won 11 national championships and have been in more bowls than a Caesar Salad.

Of the other college teams my favorite is the IPFW Mastodons, both because my wife went to that college and because I like mastodons. Don't get me wrong: I wouldn't want them around today. Deer on the roads are bad enough; imagine hitting a hairy elephant.

Oh, the oaken bucket? Indiana and Purdue Universities are the main state schools, and as happens, they ended up in a rivalry. But they wanted to mess with peoples' heads, so they took a bucket (oak, duh), and ringed it with metallic I's and P's, so it would look more or less like a trophy. Now, every football season, the schools fight it out for the right to have the old oaken bucket for another year.

Honestly, the thing's kinda ugly.

Wait, is caving a sport?

Many years of dripping water leaves mineral deposits like these in the Squire Boon caverns, which could have been fixed by a good plumber. Remember: stalactites stick tight to the ceiling, stalagmites might have, but didn't.

If caving isn't a sport, it should be … and so should competitive plumbing.

Chapter Fifteen

CRIME AND PUNS

Some people say a Hoosier's accent is a crime; I've never noticed we have an accent.

Still, we had the KKK, and we had politicians, so it goes without saying we've had other kinds of crime, too. In fact, Indiana can boast the first famous outlaw gang in the country, the Reno Gang.

Maybe "boast" isn't the right word.

Reno Isn't Just a City in Nevada

For the most part the Reno Gang consisted of four brothers: Frank, Simeon, John, and Ringo. No, not Ringo—William. Their last names were, naturally, Reno, and they were raised in Rockford, a little town north of Seymour, another little town. This is about halfway between Indianapolis and Louisville, Kentucky, which are not little towns.

As a whole the Reno's were religious farmers, but all but one of the children turned out, perhaps in their own form of rebellion, to be pretty wild. That includes their only daughter, Laura, which left only "Honest Clint" Reno to be the white sheep of the generation.

In the 1840s the four bad brothers branched out from farming into a rash of burglaries and horse thefts, and after the turn of the decade padded their portfolio with arson. When the Civil War began, recruiting officers from the north paid Frank and John a bounty to join the army, which would have settled them right down if they'd actually joined the army.

Instead, they took the money and ran. Then they went to another recruiting office, signed up, and deserted again. Later in the war, when a draft was instituted, rich draftees could hire someone else to take their place in the army. The Reno boys, having become veterans of joining the army by this point, would take their money from the draftees and disappear.

The war was good to them.

Near the end of the conflict the two returned to Rockford and formed a gang, which included two of their other brothers and some other less than savory characters. They made their hideout, perhaps ironically, in a burned out building, although history doesn't say whether they did the burning.

It was on. They robbed the post office and a store in nearby Jonesville, got caught by U.S. Marshals, posted bail, and promptly robbed two more post offices (Dudleytown and Seymour). A wave of burglaries swept through the area, too.

A man named Grant Wilson agreed to testify against the Reno boys, but, coincidentally, he turned up dead.

Armed robberies followed, along with counterfeiting, blackmailing, threatening, and jaywalking. In 1866, the headless body of a Seymour hotel guest turned up floating in the White River. That happened to be the same hotel, the Radar House, where the gang took up residence.

But the Reno's weren't content to rest on their ill-gotten laurels. They came up with a new idea: "Let's rob a train! It's never been done!"

(It had, but as a Civil War espionage operation, rather than for profit.)

On October 6, 1866, John and Simeon Reno and Frank Sparks boarded an Ohio & Mississippi train at the Seymour depot, and robbed it of $12,000. It was, indeed, the first recorded peacetime train robbery, and it happened right here in good ol' Indiana.

A postscript: The next year Walker Hammond and Michael Colleran pulled a copycat train robbery, also at Seymour, and got away with $8,000.

Sorry, I lost my train of thought

No, this isn't from the train the Reno Gang robbed ... as far as I know. This caboose obviously obeyed the stop sign by the 1895 Madison Railroad depot, and never got going again. Or, it's part of the museum display.

Incensed at being copied, John Reno tracked the two men down, beat them, and turned them into the law.

Although by the time they reached the arms of the law, Hammond and Colleran no longer had the eight thousand bucks.

With the heat on in Indiana, two of the gang traveled to Daviess County, Missouri, and robbed the courthouse there. It put John Reno on the radar of the famed Pinkerton Detective Agency (not literally—radar came later). The Pinkertons tracked John down, which got him sentenced to 25 years hard labor in the Show Me State.

Frank Reno stayed busy pulling off crimes in Indiana, but after a while he and other gang members decided to take a little vacation. They robbed three Iowa county treasuries until detective William Pinkerton caught up with them in Council Bluffs, Iowa. That got them stuck securely in a jail cell.

At least they stayed secure until, on April 1, 1868, they dug a hole in the wall and escaped. They left a note: "April Fools".

A sense of humor is always helpful.

The gang's next train robbery was in Marshfield, in south central Indiana, where they got away with $96,000. In today's cash, that's … let's see … carry the five … a lot.

The gang split the money, and also split the gang, but in the end it didn't do them much good. Six members tried to rob a train near Brownstown, west of Seymour, and broke into the express car … where ten Pinkerton detectives waited.

That proved the beginning of the end for the Reno Gang. The train transporting three members to prison was held up (ironically) west of Seymour, by the hooded Jackson County Vigilance Committee. The three soon swung from a tree, and not in a party kind of a way.

The Jackson County Vigilance Committee was made up of vigilantes from Jackson County, naturally, who were thoroughly tired of the lawlessness going on around them. They decided to fight it with … lawlessness. Wearing scarlet masks—which set them off from the white-hooded KKK—they polished up their ropes, practiced their noose tying, and went to work. I mean, they figuratively polished their ropes. You don't polish ropes, duh.

You don't, do you?

Three more Reno Gang members were tracked to Illinois and brought to Seymour by train, which must have seemed like a terrible idea. They also got stopped, and lynched from the very same tree.

William and Simeon Reno remained at large, but not for long: the Pinkertons caught them in Indianapolis and took them to the Scott County Jail. Laura Reno paid to have her brothers transferred to the New Albany Jail—she wanted her brothers in a more secure facility not to keep them from breaking out, but to keep others from breaking in.

Meanwhile, in Canada, brother Frank and a compatriot tried twice to have Alan Pinkerton killed, while Pinkerton tried to get them extradited. When that failed they tried bribery and politics (I repeat myself) but it didn't work. Frank ended up reunited with Simeon and William. The remains of the gang wrote to a Fort Wayne newspaper and threatened that if the boys hanged, all of Seymour would be burned to the ground.

Their jailer, Sheriff Fullenlove (no, I did NOT make that up), responded by swearing the Jackson County Vigilance Committee posed absolutely no danger to his prisoners.

He was wrong.

Fifty Committee members showed up. They beat Fullenlove (seriously, that's his name.) and shot him in the arm when he refused to give up the jail keys. Fullenlove (seriously!) stopped refusing.

At 4:30 that morning three of the brothers stopped breathing, along with a fourth member of the gang. Thousands of people showed up to view the bodies, and not in a mourning kind of a way, until the desperados were buried in the (unburned) Seymour City Cemetery.

No member of the Jackson County Vigilante Committee was ever arrested. This might have to do with their threats against anyone who might testify against them ... after all, they still had a supply of rope and scarlet hoods.

The last outlaw brother, John, died at home years later, after serving two prison terms for various offenses. Laura later married and became "respectable", while "Honest" Clint died in a Topeka, Kansas insane asylum. The white sheep never got arrested, except for assault and battery, selling liquor to a minor, and keeping a gambling house.

Clearly, honest is relative.

In addition to a documentary, two movies were made about the Reno Brothers: One, *Rage at Dawn* in 1955, starred Plainfield native Forrest Tucker as Frank Reno.

The other, a 1956 film, was about "Honest" Clint Reno, played by Elvis Presley: *Love Me Tender*.

Serial Killer for Breakfast

In the interest of balance, women can be bad guys, too. For instance, Belle Gunness, born in Norway, moved in 1901 to La Porte, Indiana. I skipped over her time in Chicago, where she and her husband collected the insurance from her mysteriously burned down confectionery before he also died, coincidentally on a day his two life insurance policies overlapped.

That kind of thing.

But she moved to a La Porte home, where her boat house and carriage house soon burned down. It was tragic for Belle, who had already lost two children to mysterious illnesses, but she rallied and married a man named

Peter Gunness. He already had a daughter, but she sadly died of mysterious causes while alone with Belle.

A year later Peter, Belle's new husband, got into a terrible accident. It involved scalding brine, or possibly a sausage grinding machine that fell on his skull, or maybe both.

That merited an investigation, which cleared Gunness of wrongdoing. After all, Bell was pregnant, and a pregnant woman wouldn't do horrible things like that.

By the time Belle's headless body turned up in her burning house in 1908, her little Indiana farm was littered with bodies—somewhere between two dozen and forty, over the course of several decades. And just for fun, I should add she was never positively identified ... in fact, two people who knew her insisted she was Esther Carleson, who poisoned a man for his money in Los Angeles, 13 years after she "died".

Lions and tigers and kids, oh yum!

This tiger at the Fort Wayne Children's Zoo found it greatly amusing to stalk along the wall out of sight, then suddenly appear in the window to give the kids a thrill. He did it several times as we watched, making them scream each time. Or maybe he wasn't amused, so much as hungry ...

(This chapter has nothing to do with zoos, unless you count prison ... but I figured after gangs and serial killers, we needed a palate cleanser. I'm open to throwing crooks to the lions, though)

Prohibition started in 1920, and made for a financial boon to bad guys who supplied illegal liquor to Indiana cities, despite the efforts of the Ku Klux Klan to enforce the law and stop the criminals.

Yeah, you heard right. All things considered, I'd rather have the bootleggers.

So along came organized crime, or gangs, led by gangsters like John Dillinger. Unlike the Reno Brothers, and definitely unlike Belle Gunness, and *really* definitely not like the KKK, Dillinger had a certain amount of style and charm. I mean, Johnny Depp played him in a movie. How style and charmish is that?

John Herbert Dillinger came into this world in Indianapolis, the son of a grocer who was, by all accounts, not a nice guy. I'm not saying John was messed up from an early age, but his mother died when he was three, and five years later his father married a woman John didn't like very much. Years after that he came to love his stepmother so much that they had a three year affair.

Actually, I *am* saying John Dillinger was messed up from an early age.

"Hey, Kid ... Gimmie Your Lunch Money."

Young Dillinger was a bully and a thief, who liked to fight. You know, I take back what I said earlier about his charm. His father, wanting to calm Dillinger down before he did something crazy like have an affair with his stepmother, moved the family to Mooresville in 1921. It didn't help: The next year Dillinger got arrested for auto theft.

So Dillinger joined the Navy and was assigned to the battleship *Utah*, until he deserted and came back to Mooresville. Strike two.

Then he met the woman who might settle him down, Beryl Ethel Hovious. (I'm pretty sure her name is also the chemical name of something with alcohol in it.)

It didn't work. Within a few weeks of his wedding to the sixteen-year-old, he got caught stealing chickens. Strike three.

When Dillinger and a friend robbed a local grocery store, he was recognized and arrested. Daddy Dillinger convinced his kid to confess, expecting a lenient sentence. Unfortunately, Dillinger had clobbered a victim and also shot off a gun, which impressed the judge to no end.

On his way to the Indiana Reformatory, Dillinger was diagnosed with gonorrhea. The guy couldn't catch a break, so he fell in with other criminals and learned how to give the breaks, if he couldn't catch them.

But Dillinger managed to get paroled, just after his stepmother died and during the worst of the Great Depression. What could go wrong?

"I Wanna Open an Account, Where's My Toaster?"

On June 21, 1933, Dillinger robbed his first bank, in New Carlisle, Ohio, then went on to a Bluffton bank, then to a Dayton arrest and a Lima jail cell. Seriously, nothing good comes out of travel to Ohio. Well, nothing except his first successful escape.

Dillinger's first gang, who claimed to be Indiana State Police officers, came to "extradite" Dillinger, which they did by way of killing the Sheriff when he asked for credentials.

A lot of bank robberies happened after that.

Back in Indiana, Dillinger was caught after he robbed an East Chicago bank, then jailed in Crown Point. The police there bragged the Crown Point jail was escape proof, which was really stupid. According to most reports, Dillinger used a fake pistol carved from a potato. There's more than corn in Indiana.

Dillinger left the state for a while, and I'm sure nothing interesting happened to him while he was gone. Sure, he robbed a bank in Sioux Falls, South Dakota, and for a time joined Baby Face Nelson's gang before moving into a Chicago apartment with his main squeeze, Billie. There he almost got caught, but he had a Thompson submachine gun and they didn't.

So Dillinger fled back to Indiana, and in Mooresville got into in a car accident, of all things. The police were hot on his tail, and I don't mean that literally, although it might have felt that way. When his girlfriend Billie was arrested the gang took a Warsaw police officer hostage, stealing guns and bulletproof vests as part of what may have been an attempt to break her out. But sadly, the two never saw each other again, and Dillinger went back to Chicago to lay low.

And by laying low I mean he commonly attended Chicago Cubs games.

What else he did I couldn't say, but a madam in a Gary, Indiana brothel later gave police information on who he spent time with, and it wasn't Billie. The, um, brothelette wore a bright dress when she later exited a Chicago movie theater with Dillinger.

That clued the cops in on Dillinger's identity, and the movie ended with a bang. Several, in fact.

There are many other Indiana criminals and unusual crimes, of course, just like in any other state. These are the highlights ... or maybe lowlights? But dwelling on bad guys can be bad, so we'll move on to someone who was, by all accounts, very good.

Indiana Facts:
AS HOOSIER AS APPLE PIE

You don't get more Hoosier than Johnny Appleseed, who wandered around Indiana with a pot on his head, and was buried in Fort Wayne (after the wandering, and presumably without the pot).

Or not.

After all, Johnny was born in 1774, and a lot of lore has arisen since then about him and his pot use. He's become a legend, right up there with Paul Bunyon and Babe the Blue Ox, the latter of which only appeared after the pot had been used.

The guy's real name was John Chapman, but you don't build a legend out of a regular name like that. Would heroic train engineer Casey Jones have been as famous with the name Bill Jones? (Actually, his name was Jonathon Jones, so there you go.)

To place him in history, John Chapman's father served in the Continental Army during the American Revolution. John was born in Massachusetts, at a home along Johnny Appleseed Lane, which I can only assume didn't have that name at the time. John and his younger brother went west in 1792, wandering around until the rest of the family moved to Ohio thirteen years later. That's when John became an apprentice to a Mr. Crawford, a manly orchardist. In other words, he grew apples.

Apples pretty much had to show up in the story at some point.

Johnny Appleseed did not wander the countryside, tossing apple seeds the way other people spit out sunflower seeds (and—ew). What he actually did was plant nurseries: Places where apple trees could grow until they got big enough to be useful, kind of like kids, except a lot of kids never actually become useful.

Johnny would build fences around the nurseries to keep the animals out, then leave the nurseries to a neighbor who would sell the trees. He started out in Pennsylvania, then moved on to Ohio, but you can guess where he ended up by the fact that he's in this book.

But Johnny Appleseed was also a missionary, spreading the word of The New Church, also called Swedenborgianism. I think we all know why they went by The New Church. The church was started by Emanuel Swedenborg—there's a name—who claimed to receive new revelations from Jesus during continuous visions that, so far as I know, had nothing to do with Johnny's pot.

Swedenborg taught love and charity, and Johnny took up the cause. He cared for animals and admired the Native Americans, who generally admired him right back. He also became a vegetarian, which wasn't a big thing back then.

Basically, Johnny Appleseed was a hippie.

As for the pot, it was tin and, by all accounts, he really did go around with it on his head. Why? Well, have you ever tried to cook your mush in a pot made of twigs and leaves? I didn't think so.

Nobody seems to know for sure when John Chapman died. *Harper's New Monthly Magazine* claimed he passed away in 1847, but many Indiana newspapers say he expired in 1845, and they should know: He died in Fort Wayne.

By then Johnny Appleseed was famous throughout the Midwest for spreading the gospels of God and apples, for the strange way he dressed, and for the fact that he had a well-off family in Cleveland, but lived in poverty himself. He was as well known for being barefoot as for being relentlessly cheerful.

Death and burial in Indiana gives you Indiana cred. But where exactly is Johnny Appleseed buried? Some developers claimed his grave is marked by a rock at the Canterbury Green apartment complex and golf course, which would perhaps be ironic. Johnny would have questioned why all that good apple growing land would be used for people who just walk around with a stick, cursing.

It seems more likely the stone marks where he died, at a cabin owned by the Worth family. Researchers believe he's actually buried in Johnny Appleseed Park, which seems way more appropriate ... although, again, I assume it wasn't called that at the time. When an iron fence was erected at the location, the Archer Graveyard, people were still alive who remembered his burial.

John Chapman left behind over 1,200 acres of nurseries, including four plots in Allen County around Fort Wayne. There's also a Johnny Appleseed Festival at the appropriately named park every year, and Fort Wayne's minor league baseball team is called the Tin Caps.

I think Johnny would prefer to be remembered for the nurseries.

Paul Bunyon would have been buried here, but he wouldn't fit.

Maybe it was inevitable that Johnny Appleseed's final resting place would be at Johnny Appleseed Park, at a little knoll on the north side of Fort Wayne. Yes, there are apple trees there, and it's a lovely place.

Within seed-spitting distance is the vast complex of the Allen County War Memorial Coliseum, northeast Indiana's largest and busiest event center. (Among other things, it's where the Fort Wayne Komets hockey team plays ... plus, there's roller derby. Not at the same time, although what an idea!) I wondered, while standing by Johnny's grave, how many of the tens of thousands of people there even knew an American legend was laid to rest so close by.

Chapter Sixteen:

IT'S A DISASTER, BUT AT LEAST IT'S NATURAL

It's possible Fort Wayne has the honor of being the only city in which a U.S. President helped sandbag a dike during a major flood.

Of course, Ronald Reagan was 70 years old at the time, so he only threw a handful of sandbags. Besides, I can't help thinking the residents of Fort Wayne would have preferred some other community have the particular honor of almost losing their entire city to a hundred year flood.

Most natural disasters in Indiana seem to stem from rain, wind, or my particular favorite, snow. In the case of Fort Wayne in 1982, the snow melt and spring rains came together to drown the city, which was saved partially by schoolkids given time off school to help with the sandbagging operation. Thousands of volunteers worked for days, and although some neighborhoods ended up underwater, Fort Wayne earned the nickname of "The City That Saved Itself".

But it wasn't the first time Fort Wayne saved itself.

It Really Wasn't So Great

During the Great Flood of 1913, fourteen states went through such terrible flooding it should have been called the Terrible Flood. But, in the greater sense, "great" means huge, and it was that. Over four days more than nine inches of rain fell in southern Indiana, with half of it on March 25.

As if that wasn't bad enough, March is already a prime time for water levels to be high because of snow runoff. (The flood that almost drowned Fort Wayne in 1982 happened in March; Reagan visited on March 16.)

As if *that* wasn't bad enough, the storm system which brought the flood announced itself with a tornado (at least one), which hit Terre Haute on March 23. That's the 1913 flood, mind you. Reagan didn't visit Indiana that time, and seeing as how he'd just celebrated his second birthday, he wouldn't have been of much help, anyway.

The runoff into rivers and lakes resulted in floods all over southern, central, and northeast Indiana. Between 100-200 people died in the Hoosier state alone. With over a thousand dead across the country, it became the second worst flood in U.S. history (behind the 1889 Johnstown Flood—don't even get me started on that). The Wabash River, which around Vincennes is normally about six feet deep, grew to be almost seven miles across.

Back then much disaster relief was handled by state and local governments, while other organizations helped out, including the Rotary Club. There was also a small organization that started operations in 1881, and in this crisis helped in half a dozen counties: The American Red Cross.

What, Again?

Some records you hope aren't made to be broken, but almost a century later, in 2008, some of those 1913 records were indeed shattered. In June so much rain fell that central and southern Indiana was inundated, along with neighboring states. Looting was reported in Seymour, some flood crests beat the 1913 total, and in Edinburgh almost eleven inches of rain fell in seven hours. Hundreds of thousands evacuated, and damage estimates topped a billion dollars. And all that after a century of flood control efforts.

If you live outside of Washington, D.C., a billion dollars is a fair amount of money.

Don't Know Why, There's No Sun up in the Sky

I survived the Blizzard of '78. I also survived the Blizzard of '91, '99, 2004, 2007, 2008 2009, 2011, the little ice age of the early 80s, and another one I don't remember much because I spent the whole event on a couch with strep throat. It's the first time I was ever happy to be sick.

Really, if you've seen one blizzard, you've seen all the reasons to move south. But the Blizzard of '78 was exceptional, and is rightly called the "Great Blizzard", as opposed to the others, which were only the "Awful Blizzards". I really did have an "I Survived the Blizzard of '78" t-shirt, but at the time it wasn't all that funny.

Also called the White Hurricane, it gave us the lowest non-tropical atmospheric pressure ever recorded in the continental U.S., a record not beaten until 2010. It roared across the Ohio Valley like a big white wall of misery, in late January.

Temperatures dropped to zero, winds peaked past 50 mph, and 10-20 foot snow drifts closed every single road in Indiana. "Whiteout conditions" is a fancy way of saying you couldn't see your own hand, aided by the fact that your hand turned an icy blue. Three feet of snow dropped on the ironically named South Bend.

Wind chill factors dropped to minus 40-50 degrees, and I'll remind you wind chill is just an expression of how horribly miserable you are and is being a beach bum in New Orleans so bad?

Excuse me, I'm off for some hot chocolate.

Toto, Kansas Isn't So Bad, After All

Weather Indiana is in Tornado Alley depends on who you ask, unless you ask a Hoosier. (Weather—see what I did, there?) We know very well we're within the alley, or at least within a few feet of being mugged by every supercell storm system that floats by.

It's no surprise, then, that we were involved in the deadliest tornado outbreak in U.S. history, the Tri-State tornado of 1925.

On March 18, 295 people were killed—more than twice as many as in the second deadliest, the 1840 Great Natchez Tornado. The Tri-State made the longest tornado track ever recorded. The twister touched down in southeastern Missouri, rampaged through southern Illinois, and then entered southwest Indiana before it finally faded away. Worse, at least a dozen other tornadoes struck that day, as if one wasn't enough.

We also have the Palm Sunday tornado outbreak ... or rather *outbreaks*. There were three: 1920, 1965, and 1994. The first two dropped funnels in Indiana, as well as several other states ... in fact, the first two spawned tornadoes in counties neighboring the one I grew up and live in.

It would take a whole book to describe the havoc tornadoes have brought to Indiana, not to mention this volume is supposed to be more funny than disaster-y. But I have to mention the disaster that most affected me personally: the one so big they call it the Super Outbreak.

On April 3-4, 1974, came the second largest tornado outbreak ever (the biggest followed in April, 2011). It remains the most violent, with 30 tornadoes rated at F4 or F5. 148 tornadoes were confirmed in 13 states and Ontario. At one point 15 tornadoes reached the ground at the same time.

Four people were killed in my county, Noble. As an 11 year old boy, I stood out in the back yard a couple of miles away, wondering why the sky turned such a vivid, sickly green. We lived out in the country and didn't have alert scanners back then.

I was seeing the effects of the longest lasting tornado of the Super Outbreak. It crossed almost the entire state on a 121 mile track, which started in Benton County and ended in Noble County. Its damage path was investigated by Ted Fujita, whose last name is the "F" in the tornado severity scale.

Since then I've spotted a few funnel clouds, but never saw one actually touch down. Some of us are just lucky like that.

It's a twister! It's a twister!
Ask a Hoosier if Indiana is in Tornado Alley, and be prepared for a windy response. This funnel was captured by me along I-69, near the DeKalb-Steuben County border, in 2015. Then I went home to change my underwear.

Shake, Rattle and Roll

Thank goodness, there are certain natural disasters that don't impact Indiana, such as hurricanes and earthquakes.

I mean, except for how that's not true.

At least five hurricanes have affected Indiana in a big way. By the time they got here, they were no longer hurricanes—more like really big thunderstorms that dropped a lot of rain and some lightning on us. Still, it counts.

Don't believe they'd have an impact this far in? Well, in 1959 Hurricane Debra not only dumped flooding rain on Indiana, it sparked thunderstorms that in turn started wildfires—in Montana and Idaho. Hurricane Ike brought unusually strong wind gusts to northern Indiana, Arlene dropped 4.44 inches of rain on Evansville and at least two tornadoes in other parts of the state, and Grace graced us with 9 inches of rain, flooding much of Indianapolis.

At least we don't have to worry about earthquakes.

Well, other than the 1811-12 New Madrid earthquakes that would have caused major damage in Indiana if there's been anything here to damage at the time. And the 1895 earthquake that did damage buildings in Evansville. And the 1909 Wabash River Valley quake felt across eight states. And the 1987, 1937, 1958, 1968 ...

On the brighter side, there are always volcanoes.

Okay, I just checked and you can relax: No volcanoes in Indiana. Well, not in recorded history. If we survived 2012, we'll probably be okay.

Indiana Facts:

CULTURE'S NOT JUST FOR TEST TUBES ANYMORE

I'm a big fan of fine art, although I don't understand it at all. After all, I'm also a big fan of women, and according to my wife I don't understand them, either.

One writes humor about something one doesn't understand at one's peril. (See how I got all arty, there?) For instance, impressionist painting got big in Indiana, but I can't get an impression of when it's good or bad.

Wow, that flag whipped around just in a nick of time
See the naked man? His name is Pro Patria, and at 24 feet tall and seven tons, he was the largest cast bronze sculpture in the United States. But he's almost 90 now, so it's possible he shrunk a little. Just the same, the statue, designed by Henry Hering, proudly and shamelessly guards the Indiana War Memorial in downtown Indy.

So we won't go into great detail on the history of the arts in Indiana, except to say there was some.

Literature I'm on somewhat less shaky ground with. To be literary, a novel must have no plot and an unhappy ending. See how easy that was?

Indiana had a golden age of literature, which some pundits say lasted from the late 1800s into the 1920s. After that it was replaced by The Lone Ranger on the radio, which itself was replaced, ironically, by The Lone Ranger on TV.

It started in 1871, when *The Hoosier Schoolmaster* by Edward Eggleston became the first best seller from Indiana. A number of famous writers followed along, including Booth Tarkington, James Whitcomb Riley, and Lew Wallace, who penned (perhaps literally) *Ben Hur*. Contrary to popular belief, that novel was not written by Charlton Heston.

Indiana-made music and painting also got big at this time, including a group of painters who became known as the Hoosier Group. They were famous for colorful Indiana landscapes, and to this day our landscapes can be pretty darned cool. The names Steele, Stark, Adams, Forsyth, and Gruelle were among those famous for talking painting, teaching painting, exhibiting painting, and just generally painting.

Brown County, which includes the town of Nashville and is renowned for its fall colors, hosted an art colony in the early 1900s, and to this day embraces its title of "The Art Colony of the Midwest". While I don't know who gets the naming rights in this case, I can tell you Brown County is pretty darned art inspiring.

On the subject of art, we'll mention again Paul Dressler, whose most popular song was turned into the official state song of Indiana: "On the Banks of the Wabash, Far Away". This will come as a shock to fans of the Indianapolis 500, but "Back Home Again in Indiana" didn't make the cut.

Architecture's also an art. It's Scottish, Rite?

A 1996 Indianapolis Business Journal poll found the Scottish Rite Cathedral to be the most popular historic building in the city. That's amazing, considering the number of other historic buildings just sitting around, waiting to be voted on.

Every dimension of this 1927 building, when measured in feet, is evenly divisible by three. It's one of those things the Masons do, and the Valley of Indianapolis Scottish Rite is indeed affiliated with Freemasonry. It's one of the largest Masonic buildings, and—let's face it—it's just neat.

Chapter Seventeen

PARKS AND RECREATION

(IT SOUNDED LIKE A GOOD TITLE, SO I STOLE IT.)

At one time taking a break in Indiana meant poking the fireplace logs for a few minutes at bedtime. Maybe after dinner Pa would take out his fiddle and play a merry tune, or maybe I stole that from Laura Ingalls Wilder, but there was little time for play once all the work and chores got done. (Chores are like work, but without the pay.)

Hunting and fishing were work. If you didn't get the main course, the family meal of flour cake and grass from the back yard just wouldn't be the same.

But times change, and by 1849 the first conservation law came to Indiana when Green County made it illegal to poison fish. Yeah, you gotta eat, but you can see how throwing poison into the same pond you have to fish from tomorrow—and maybe drink from—might be a self-defeating prospect. Also, did it never occurred to people that if they eat the fish they poisoned, they might get ... poisoned?

In 1881 the State Legislature created the Office of Commissioner of Fisheries, which despite its name is far from the smelliest thing politicians have ever done. Eight years later, realizing a commissioner in an office wasn't all that helpful alone, the State gave county road commissioners the authority to enforce fish and game laws.

Road commissioners. I have no explanation.

Game wardens came along in 1911, and ten years later they set a national record in arrests. Today they're called State Conservation Officers, and I once got the opportunity to see them in basic training: I would *not* mess with those people.

A Conservative Viewpoint

In 1919 the Indiana Department of Conservation came along, and we now shorten that to DNR. Wait, what? No, not Do Not Resuscitate—Department of Natural Resources. It just sounds more ... cool.

Today the DNR maintains about two dozen state parks, the largest in Brown County and the second largest being the Indiana Dunes State Park, which would just about have to be up where the dunes are. Marion and Clark counties, not to be outdone by size, each have two state parks.

The goal was to have at least one state park within an hour's drive of any Hoosier (or at least, any Hoosier who happens to be in Indiana). That was met when Prophetstown State Park came along in 2004, although one can argue it depends on how fast a Hoosier drives. The newest park is a mile east of the site of the Battle of Tippecanoe, which shows something interesting about Hoosier State Parks: They're not only recreational areas, but areas of history and natural wonders.

It's not Niagara, but it's still cool
Just one of the four waterfalls at Clifty Falls State Park will make you think you're not in flat old Indiana anymore. Much of southern Indiana is rugged, having not been scoured by ancient glaciers, and this area near the Ohio River is about as rugged as it gets. The views change with the weather and seasons, but never get less than spectacular.

But the first was McCormick's Creek State Park, dedicated on July 4, 1916, as part of Indiana's centennial celebration. We've mentioned it before, sort of: It's named after John Wesley McCormick, who claimed a hundred acres there in 1816. Another John Wesley McCormick—Junior—settled in the middle of White River State Park, becoming the first resident of what would someday be Indianapolis. Um, there was no White River State Park there at the time.

John Jr. built a tavern nearby. I mean, later he did, when other people arrived for him to drink with. In June, 1820, a meeting was held in that very tavern to decide the permanent location of Indiana's capital. The capital was in Corydon at the time, but it's no coincidence that Indianapolis was laid out in the general neighborhood of Junior's tavern.

Turkey Run State Park came along same year as McCormick's Creek, and one can only assume turkeys ran there

Park it Here

The first naturalist program in the entire country began at McCormick's Creek State Park, in 1927. I just wanted to throw that in there, because Indiana more often than not is more into middles than firsts.

Our parks were originally about natural environments—like the cliffs and falls of Clifty Falls (I see what they did, there), and the kettle lakes of my favorite, Chain O' Lakes State Park. But later they expanded to take in historical locations like Mounds State Park, which no, isn't related to the candy bar. Unless that's where the Native Americans dumped their wrappers?

They also now have places purely for recreational purposes, and there's nothing wrong with that. One of the signs of civilization is when people don't have to live in tents and cook over fires, but still choose to do it voluntarily.

I didn't want to go in, but I caved
A view of freedom from deep inside a cave at Clifty Falls State Park. The park's name hints at cliffs and falls, but it also has some pretty spectacular holes in the ground—not to mention views of the Ohio River.

Want to freeze half to death in lake and stream water? Canoe in circles while screaming at your partner to paddle on the other side? Cast a fish hook into a willow tree? Break your leg skiing in the winter and your elbow biking in the summer? Ride a horse that may or may not be comparing your size to his while he wonders who should really be in charge?

You can do at least one of those things in every park, and all in some of them. My personal favorite is the trails; I love hiking, and there are hundreds upon hundreds of hiking trails through all sorts of terrain across the state. I know what you're thinking: Why walk when you can ride?

I don't know.

Here's just a sample of parks:

- Falls of the Ohio is a park that overlooks the Falls of the Ohio, not to mention Louisville, Kentucky.
- Fort Harrison was created from old Fort Benjamin Harrison.
- Indiana Dunes is at the Indiana Dunes, along Lake Michigan.
- Lincoln is across from the Lincoln Boyhood National Memorial.
- Tippecanoe River and White River State Parks are along ... well, you know.
- Potato Creek ... I got nothin' on that one. We spent the day there twice, and never saw a single potato.

This place is for the birds

A hawk, or an egret, or maybe a vampire bat, looks over its manor at Potato Creek State Park. Birders are thrilled that bald eagles, of which this is not one, are becoming more common in Indiana. Drivers are not thrilled that wild turkeys are also making a comeback. (Editor's note: It's an osprey.)

Historical Museum History

These days you can't swing an historical artifact without hitting a museum in Indiana, although they frown on swinging the artifacts, so don't. But back in 1870 the state geologist set aside a display case in his board room for specimens of birds and mammals. Not a room, just a case.

This case became a room in the old statehouse, and that turned into the Indiana State Museum, which now resides in the White River State Park in downtown Indy. It's a Big Deal.

Now we have museums to conserve art, cars, glass, aircraft, sports, writing, and my favorite, fire apparatus. (Actually, my favorite is the Old Jail Museum in Albion, which is indeed in an old jail, and just a short walk from my home.)

There are so many museums it's beyond the scope of this work to list them all, which is another way of saying there are only so many jokes to make about each individually.

And Other Stuff

If you plan to recreate in Indiana—and who doesn't?—there's lot of other stuff if you're not the outdoorsy type. Maybe you're outdoorsy, but not enough to tramp around in turkey territory. Don't we all sometimes feel like we've spent enough time around turkeys? Well, there are fairs and festivals all over the place, from spring through autumn. There's also cross country skiing in winter, which goes to show we Hoosiers try to give crazy people something to do.

If you think outdoor people are crazy all year round, there are wineries for the snooty, casinos for the less than snooty, and the Hair Museum of French Lick for the morbidly curious. Well, *I'm* curious.

Okay: it's a "walk through hair styling history". I'm still interested, and what does that say about me? (They have a lock of Elvis Presley's hair!)

There are plenty of places for the kiddies, such as Science Central in Fort Wayne, and the Children's Museum in Indianapolis, which I haven't been to, but assume is for children. There's Holiday World, but there's also the Atlantis Water Park (in southern Indiana, not Atlantis), and Indiana Beach (which is in Indiana, along a beach). I can tell you from experience you must ride Indiana Beach's Steel Hawg. It has the world's first "outside" turn, which I can describe best with the word "terrifying". For a short time the Steel Hawg was the world's steepest roller coaster. Did I mention terrifying?

There's a Beach, and it's in Indiana, So ...
Indiana Beach is one of several amusement parks, large and small, across Indiana. The amusement resort and waterpark opened along Lake Shafer in 1926, and became the largest attraction of its kind in the state. The Shafer Queen Paddlewheel boat is a great way to recover from more than three dozen other rides, which go way faster.

This Place is a Zoo, But Enough about Politics

I don't know how many zoos are in Indiana; do we include the Statehouse?

(Yes, I know—two political jokes in two lines. I'm weak.)

There's the Indianapolis Zoo, which also has an aquarium and a botanical garden.

There's the Fort Wayne Children's Zoo, a favorite of mine because I used to hang out there as a child. Hey, it kept me and the tigers off the streets.

The Mesker Park Zoo in Evansville opened way back in 1928, although it's assumed none of the present animals date back that far.

The Potawatomi Zoo is even older, and is the oldest zoo in the state. But it's like a cool older zoo, not a codger zoo, yelling at you to stay off its lawn.

That's just a sample, and far from the only places to see exotic animals. Some places don't fit the definition of zoo:

By far my favorite—it started out in my home town and is now a short distance away—is Black Pine Animal Sanctuary of Albion. It's a sanctuary—a place for animals retired with no benefits, or abandoned. I used to get chills when I'd hear a lion's roar through my home's window, and by chills I mean slamming the window shut and whimpering for my mommy. I was thirty.

I'm not lion
For a close up of a hungry-looking lion, it's better to have a fence between you. Mufasa moved to Black Pine Animal Sanctuary near Albion in 2011, and is a prime example of the exotic animals to be found around the Hoosier state. He thinks of us as more of a prime meat example.

Hunting is also a big recreational activity in Indiana. Despite my name I don't hunt personally, but have benefited by way of the occasional deer steak or summer sausage. I feel it's payback for the big buck that did $1,100 damage (and that's before inflation) to the van I was driving, then stuck its tongue out at me and ran off.

Deer were once almost wiped out in Indiana, but conservation efforts brought them back with such a vengeance that they're now a common cause of accidents here. Now turkeys are starting to populate the state again; it may not sound as serious as deer, but if you ever have one of those butterballs flutter out in front of your speeding car, you'll feel it.

In addition to deer and turkey, there are seasons for hunting furbearers, small game, waterfowl, and game birds. I don't know much about them; I did try trapping for food once, but they chased me out of the grocery store.

That just scratches the surface of recreation in Indiana, and yet I've already had to apply antiseptic and a bandage. There are all sorts of outdoor and indoor facilities for all sorts of things, so if you're here, take advantage; if you're not here, why not? Except during winter—I get it during winter.

Indiana Facts:

In 1854, the little town of Santa Fe, Indiana was established, and as with all little towns the people wanted their own post office. "Hold your horses," the United States Postal Service said. Seeing as how this was 1854, that might be quite literally what they said.

Turns out they already had a Santa Fe, Indiana. The new townspeople held a series of meetings to look for the right new name, while ignoring the crazy old coot in the back who kept yelling, "Why, just change it to Santa Claus! Hee hee hee!!!"

Rumor has it the old guy in the back was, in fact, Santa Claus, which they should have figured out from his white beard, bowl full of jelly, and the giant

Santa! I _know_ him!
Surely I'm not the only person who stops to get his photo taken at the Santa Claus welcome sign. The Spencer County community has a population of about 2,481—making it almost exactly the same size as my home town, Albion. But its main attraction, Holiday World & Splashin' Safari, brings over a million visitors a year.
The former Santa Claus land changed its name because it now holds four themed sections: Christmas, Halloween, Fourth of July, and Thanksgiving. Santa, as you can see in this image, is not amused. Or maybe he's just sneezing.

soot-covered bag of toys. Using his Christmas magic, which is kind of like the

Force, he convinced the townspeople it was their idea to become residents of Santa Claus.

That might be hedging a bit on the details. But today the only post office in the world named Santa Claus is in Indiana, and over a half million letters go to this Santa Claus every year. You'd think it would be in northern Indiana, but no, the town's not all that far from the Ohio River, all the way south.

You will *never guess* what theme the town takes on year round.

Oh, you guessed! Well, in 1935 the town became the host of the Santa's Candy Castle, sponsored by Chicago's Curtiss Candy Company—which created the Butterfinger and Baby Ruth candy bars. Kinda fits.

That was the start of what became the world's first theme park. Oh, sure, there might be some town in Liechtenstein arguing they got their first with Alpine Skiing World in 1673, but did they have a giant Santa Claus statue? Or Butterfingers? I think not.

In 1946 came Santa Claus Land, which has since become Holiday World and boasts the number one wooden roller coaster on the planet—according to *Time* Magazine. In 2013 *Time* also declared the town's water park, Splashin' Safari, the country's best water park.

A water park doesn't seem very Santa Claus-y, but hey—this is his summer home, after all.

Also around town you'll find the Santa Claus Museum, Santa Claus Christmas Store, Santa's Stables, Santa's Lodge, Santa's Cottages, and Christmas Lake Golf Course, among other things. There has to be stuff for vacationing elves to do too, right?

On an incidental note, Abraham Lincoln's boyhood home is just four miles from town. Apparently that part of Indiana has a thing for beards.

Finding Santa Claus is easy: Just take State Route 162 until it magically turns into ... Christmas Boulevard.

Tell me the guy in the middle isn't the ghost of Richard Attenborough

With a town called Santa Claus in the state, you have to figure a lot of Santa's are wandering around. Sure enough, a whole herd of them showed up for the Albion Fire Department's 225th anniversary celebration, even though Albion and Santa Claus are on opposite ends of the state. (They were actually in the area for a different event, but as you'd expect with St. Nicholas, they were good sports.)

Trivial Pursuits

One famous native of Indiana is Raggedy Ann. The doll was created by Marcella Gruelle   in 1914. Marcella Gruelle, a cousin of Cruella Deville, did *not* make her dolls from puppy fur.

Crown Hill Cemetery in Indianapolis is the third largest in the world (cemetery, not hill), with over 185,000 graves on 555 acres. People are—say it with me—dying to get in.

It's south only in name

The southern shore of Lake Michigan has been turned into a paradise of sand: the Indiana Dunes State Park. Unfortunately it's the northwest tip of Indiana—or maybe fortunately, if you like lake effect snow. This dune view shows the Lake Michigan beach, historic bathhouse, and also some anonymous little city, which we don't care about because it's fifty miles across the lake, in Illinois. Chicag-something?

This park is not to be confused with the Indiana Dunes National Lakeshore ... what the heck, visit both.

In Crawfordsville you'll find the only working rotary jail in the country. Yeah, the cellblock rotates. Get that thing turning fast enough and prisoners will confess to anything.

Mount Baldy, the largest of the Indiana Dunes, moves a few feet away from the shores of

Lake Michigan every year. Possibly it's concerned about sea level rise from global warming.

With 32 of them, Parke County is the Covered Bridge Capital of the world. Again, I don't know who gives this designation. Surely there are a lot of bridges in Madison County.

Nancy Kerlin Barnett's 1831 grave can easily be found near Amity ... in fact, you have to be careful to miss it, as it's in the middle of a county road. Her son, and then grandson, objected to the grave being moved, so the county just divided their new road around the gravesite, which now has an historical marker.

You'll find lots of horse drawn buggies in northern Indiana, home to Amish and one of the largest Mennonite populations in the country.

I've joked about towns not having electricity, but in 1880 Wabash actually became the first community to get electric street lights. It was ... enlightening.

In a surprisingly unrelated fact, the largest manufacturer of horse drawn wagons in the U.S. used to be South Bend's Studebaker. They later moved on to automobiles, which proved to be a smart decision.

The first practical gasoline pump was developed in Fort Wayne, and the world has had gas ever since.

On an also surprisingly unrelated note, Indiana is where Gilbert Van Camp popularized his family pork and beans recipe, opened a canning company, and got rich.

The Circus Capital of America was once Peru, Indiana, where several circuses had winter quarters. This is also where John Dillinger once robbed a police department armory. Again, unconnected.

Speaking of Peru, in 1972 Lowell Elliot found a half million dollars in cash on his farm near town. No, it wasn't Dillinger's lost stash: It was dropped by a skyjacker, a D.B. Cooper wannabe who didn't get to be. (Since skyjacking doesn't happen much anymore, I should explain it's when an airplane gets hijacked, usually for cash or a ride to another country—or both. D.B. Cooper bailed out of a Boeing 727 in 1971 with $200,000, and was never seen again.)

A tree grows from the roof of the courthouse tower in Greenwood, over a hundred feet in the air. Hopefully it doesn't have an issue with heights, but at least it's safe from termites.

Like white-water rafting? The only artificial course for that sport in North America is in South Bend.

Indiana's first newspaper, the Indiana Gazette, came out in Vincennes in 1804. Unfortunately, no one in Vincennes could read at the time.

An unknown singer got his start with the Tommy Dorsey Orchestra in 1940 at the Lyric Theatre, in Indianapolis. Well, unknown then—his name was Frank Sinatra.

Another Frank, this one fictional and much less beloved, hails from Fort Wayne: Frank Burns, bad guy surgeon on the TV show M*A*S*H.

One of America's first female millionaires was Indiana's Sarah Walker, who developed a conditioning treatment to straighten hair. Later someone countered it with the country's first curling iron, which proved to be a miserable failure because no one yet had electricity.

The famous Coca-Cola bottle was invented in Terra Haute. I'm not sure whether they still put cocaine in their product at that point.

Ironically, I couldn't find a Coca-Cola bottle

Sure, Coke may have come from a different state—but you can't have Coca-Cola without a bottle to drink it from. Well, you could, but things might get messy. Thanks to the Root Glass Company of Terra Haute winning a national competition, you don't have to worry about getting your Coke through pipelines, straight to your kitchen tap. Or would that have been a good thing?

As mentioned earlier, Indy native Richard Gatling invented the machine gun in 1862. A couple of those guns were available years later to George Armstrong Custer, but he chose not to take them along when he left to battle the Native Americans. He should have.

Oh, and one more thing:

Indiana stole its name. "Indiana" was first applied, in fact, way back in the 1760s to a tract of land in Pennsylvania. Indiana the city is now county seat of Indiana the county, and promotes itself as Christmas Tree Capital of the World. Wouldn't it be something if they shipped some of their trees to Santa Claus?

By the way, that area is the birthplace of famous actor Jimmy Stewart; so I can say with a straight face:

Jimmy Stewart is from Indiana.

Sadly, to my knowledge there is no Pennsylvania, Indiana.

Tanks for coming!
Why throw in a photo of a Sherman tank? Because it's a friggin' Sherman tank, that's why. But also because it shows how serious the city of Huntington is about keeping their parks secure.

Chapter Eighteen

A LOVE LETTER TO INDIANA, BUT NOT IN AN ICKY KIND OF WAY

So here we are, in the 21st Century. How has Indiana changed?

In many ways it hasn't. This is something residents decry or celebrate, based largely on their position in the political spectrum.

But we are undoubtedly a different state than we were in 1816. The world still thinks of Indiana as a rural place, full of farms and the things you'd find on farms, like horses, corn, and mortgages. But Indiana has the fifth highest population density in the country, which I'd remind you consists of fifty states. The Chicago Metropolitan Area juts into Indiana, and the Indianapolis area has more than a million people.

As for me, as a kid my closest neighbors ran a hog farm a quarter of a mile away. Sometimes I miss it, depending on wind direction.

There are about six and a half million people here, now, and after 200 years only about .03% of them are Native Americans.

Although Indianapolis is the second largest city in the Midwest and the 14th largest in the country, well over a million acres of state land is used for outdoor recreation. You want great fall colors? Brown County State Park. You want waterfalls? Clifty Falls State Park. You want great fishing? Just about any place with a body of water will have someone casting a line into it. Boy, does that get annoying at bath time.

Gary is the fourth biggest city in Indiana, after Indy, Fort Wayne, and Evansville. It's up northwest in the Rust Belt, along Lake Michigan and close enough to Chicago that one of its neighbors is East Chicago. And yet, you can leave the city, dip your toes into the sands at Indiana Dunes National Lakeshore—and still see the city. Any place where they have to periodically bulldoze a dune off the parking lot is worth checking out.

While Gary's population has slipped a bit, Fort Wayne is going strong with over 250,000 people. You might remember it as the place where General Wayne built a fort, and today you can go there and see the same fort.

Okay, not the *exact* same fort ... but then, Wayne didn't build it by himself, either.

South Bend is next, and proof you don't have to go to Paris to see Notre Dame. Notre Dame is a French term meaning "Our Lady", which gives some irony to the fact that Notre Dame University's famous sports team is nicknamed the Fighting Irish. Still, it's been there since 1842, and any school named after the Virgin Mary I wouldn't dare argue with.

What's in a Name?

Some time ago I discovered my northeast Indiana hometown wasn't the only Albion in Indiana: There's a tiny crossroads of the same name in the southern end of the state. They were probably first, since the southern part of the state generally got settled first; but as a (northern) Albionite who doesn't want to admit to being second, I don't plan to pursue it.

The other Albion doesn't have one of these
As a resident of Albion, I'd be remiss if I didn't include a photo (or two) of the 1887 Noble County Courthouse, the coolest courthouse in all of Indiana's 92 counties. A few residents of other counties might be inclined to argue with me on this, but then I'd be forced to tell them they're wrong. (Historical Photo courtesy Noble County Historical Society)

It turns out duplicate town names are not at all uncommon in Indiana. There are, for instance, five Mount Pleasants, even though we don't have an official mountain. There are four Buena Vista's, a name meaning "I like this place; let's kick the Indians out". There are four Millersburgs, which is maybe not a surprise considering the number of Millers. We also have four Salems, three Hamiltons, three Wheelings and—this is my favorite—three Needmores.

Need more what? Judging from the needs of early pioneers, it could be cloth, steel plows, buttons, doctors ... but it's probably booze.

We were a new state when most of these towns got laid out, so it's no surprise 52 of Indiana's towns have "New" in the title. Another 23 have "Saint", because the pioneers needed all the help they could get.

Settlers heading west put "West" in the name of 24 towns. Those with bad senses of direction used "South" in 14, and "East" in seven. There weren't all that many Norths; go figure. However, there were 13 with some variation of "Green" ... setting out for greener pastures, after all. Finally, there are 12 towns with "Lake" in the name—two of them in Lake County.

None of this includes unincorporated towns. The first town in Noble County was Wolf Lake, but it never incorporated. The wolves left the area after it became one of the prime onion producing regions in the country; they couldn't take the scent.

There are now 92 counties in Indiana. That started with Knox County, created a full 26 years before the state itself came along. It was a *big* county. The last was in 1859 with Newton County, thus the "new" in the title. Newton had a rough time of it, as it was formed in 1835 with different borders, abolished, then recreated. Sheesh, can't you leave a county alone?

Newton and an adjoining county, Jasper, were named after sergeants who served under General Francis Marion during the Revolutionary War. Their service happened in the Carolinas and Marion never got to Indiana, so I have no explanation—but the states of Georgia, Mississippi, Missouri, and Texas also have adjacent Jasper and Newton Counties. Kinda spooky.

Although Allen County (Fort Wayne) is the largest county in size, the most populated is Marion because—Indianapolis. In both population and size the smallest is Ohio; people refused to move there because the name bothered them. (I kid—the county was actually named after the Ohio River.)

Most of our counties, like most everything else, got named after Founding Fathers, heroes of early wars, or Native American names and words. For instance, Washington County is named after ...

I really don't have to tell you, do I?

In other News ...

Indiana currently has nine U.S. Representatives, but we don't hold that against them.

Although the U.S. has never declared an official language, Indiana's is English. This probably wouldn't sit well with the Native Americans originally here, or the French who popped in from time to time. On the other hand, I've spent some time trying to pronounce American Indian words, and English ain't so bad.

We have about two dozen state parks, which occupy 56,409 acres, and seventeen state historic sites. I have a soft spot for the one at my back door, Chain O' Lakes State Park. (It's not literally at my back door, although that would be cool.) Chain O' Lakes has lakes—a whole chain of them. There are other official forests, preserves, fish and wildlife areas, and memorials across the state. Not only that, but we have the largest population of mosquitoes in the upper Midwest.

A ride in the park

A bicyclist enjoys the autumn colors at Chain O' Lakes State Park. Although Brown County is—perhaps ironically, considering the name—famed for its colorful fall foliage, it's not hard to find beautiful scenery across the state.

In 2012, Indiana's economic exports hit a record high of $34.4 billion, which is a few. Our rate of growth was faster than in the rest of the country, so in your face, rest of the country.

The second largest medical school in the country is Indiana University, and who cares who's first? Indiana has become a leader in the medical industry: If you're a driver, your chances of surviving a collision with a deer in Indiana are almost as high as your chances of actually hitting a deer.

I mean, come on: We've got both the largest and the second largest casket manufactures in the world. (30 miles apart, in Batesville and Aurora.) The rest of the competition is six feet under. Can you dig it? They buried the competition. Okay, that's enough.

Indiana remains a manufacturing state; a farming state; a recreation state; a learning state. If Indiana were a person, it would have a split personality.

We wouldn't have it any other way.

About the Authors

Mark and Emily Hunter live in small town Indiana with their loving but scary looking dog Baeowulf (the spelling's a long story), her cowardly ball python Lucius, and enough books to cause a medium-sized avalanche. He's a 911 dispatcher and volunteer firefighter, and she wrangles horses for the saddle barn at Pokagon State Park.

She also wrangles him: Together they wrote the local history books *Images of America: Albion and Noble County* and *Smoky Days and Sleepless Nights: A Century or So With the Albion Fire Department*. She also helped him produce the young adult novel *The No-Campfire Girls* and a collection of his humor columns, *Slightly Off the Mark*. Mark R Hunter also has two published romantic comedies and a short story collection in the *Storm Chaser* series. All the books are set—more or less—in Indiana.

Their works can be found at www.markrhunter.com, or on Amazon at http://www.amazon.com/Mark-R-Hunter/e/B0058CL6OO.

Made in the USA
Monee, IL
22 June 2024

60346798R10096